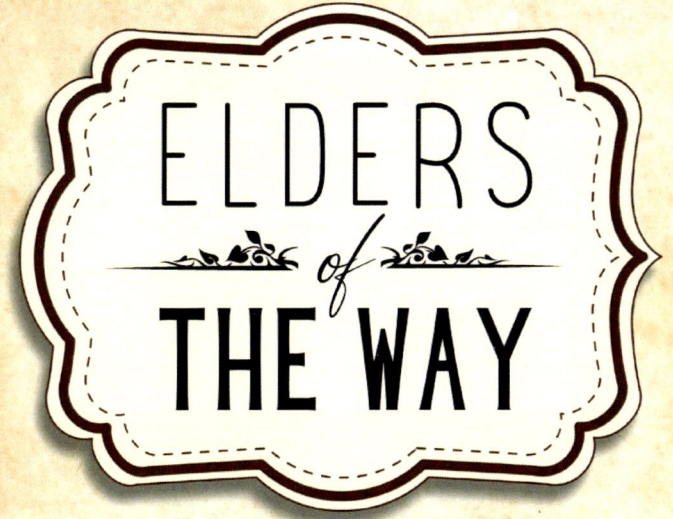

for **POP**

POPPY HARRY MUNDINE WALKER

Trust in the Lord with all your heart and lean not on your own understanding.

PROVERBS 3:5

and **MA**

AUNTY ANNABELLE WALKER

Come, let us sing for joy to the Lord; let us shout aloud to the Rock of our salvation.

PSALM 95:1

THE TIMELESS TORCH

Hello and welcome!

This book comes to you from *Elders of The Way*, a ministry and movement calling a generation to take hold of the timeless torch of faith being handed down by the elders across the globe.

A 100% non-commercial resource, it is self-published at the request of Poppy Harry Mundine Walker, our beloved founder, and *Chief Encourager* whose dream it was to get the tales and teachings found in these pages into as many hands as possible.

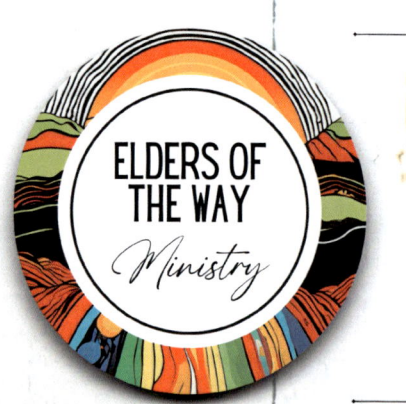

© 2024 Elders of The Way
All Rights Reserved
LCCN: 2024919888
ISBN: 979-8-9915976-0-9

---

eldersoftheway.com

ELDERS of THE WAY

An Ancient Dream Reborn

Remember your leaders, who spoke the word of God to you. Consider the outcome of their way of life and imitate their faith.

Hebrews 13:7

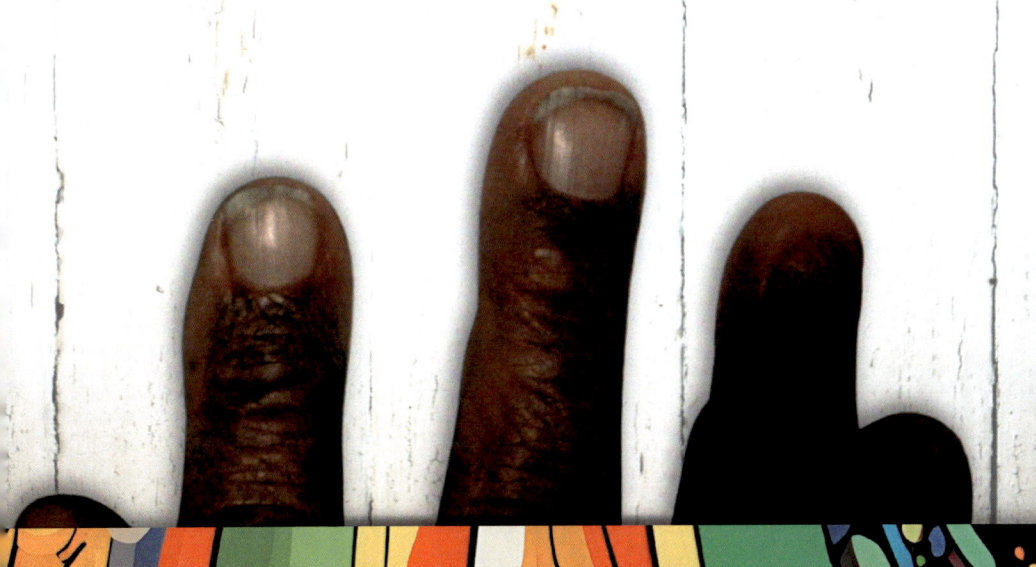

THE OLD CHURCH ON THE MISSION

JUBULLUM

CHURCH OF THE HOLY SEPULCHRE

JERUSALEM

THE STONE CHURCH AT KAWAIAHA'O

HONOLULU

① THE CALLING *Part One*

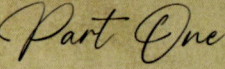

TO AMERICA

TWO BOOMERANGS

THIS FAMILY

ON HOLY GROUND

AT THE RIVER

OUT OF THE WORLD

② THE TORCH *Part Two*

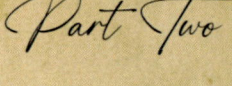

LIFE GIVING GIFT

THE SHEPHERD

OUR SUPPLY

LEGACY OF GOLD

THE REVEREND

CHIEF TO CHIEF

③ THE JOURNEY 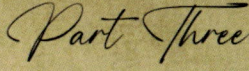 *Part Three*

THE EXODUS

THE TOMB

THE FORTRESS

THE PALACE

THE ISLANDS

THE VALLEY

④ THE DREAM 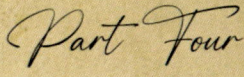 *Part Four*

IN THE BEGINNING

ENDS OF THE EARTH

OLD STONE CHURCH

ANOTHER CHORUS

ANCIENT DREAM

ACROSS THE BRIDGE

THE CALLING
Part One

Take Me to America	....	9
Two Boomerangs & A Cross	....	15
This Family Was Forever	....	21
Standing on Holy Ground	....	27
Shall We Gather at the River	....	33
Call Them Out of the World	....	39

THE TORCH
Part Two

This Life Giving Gift	....	47
Sheep for the Shepherd	....	53
The Source of Our Supply	....	59
Leaving a Legacy of Gold	....	65
To Become the Reverend	....	71
They Stood Chief to Chief	....	77

THE JOURNEY
Part Three

Exodus of the Heart	………………….	87
Tomb of the Risen One	………………	93
This Fortress of Faith	……………….	99
Meet Us At The Palace	………………	107
Islands of Living Hope	………………	115
Peace in the Valley	…………………..	121

THE DREAM
Part Four

Like in the Beginning	………………	131
At the Ends of the Earth	…………..	137
The Old Stone Church	………………	143
Sing Out Another Chorus	…………	149
An Ancient Dream Reborn	…………	155
First Across the Bridge	…………….	163

> *This is the way, walk in it.*
>
> **ISAIAH 30:21**

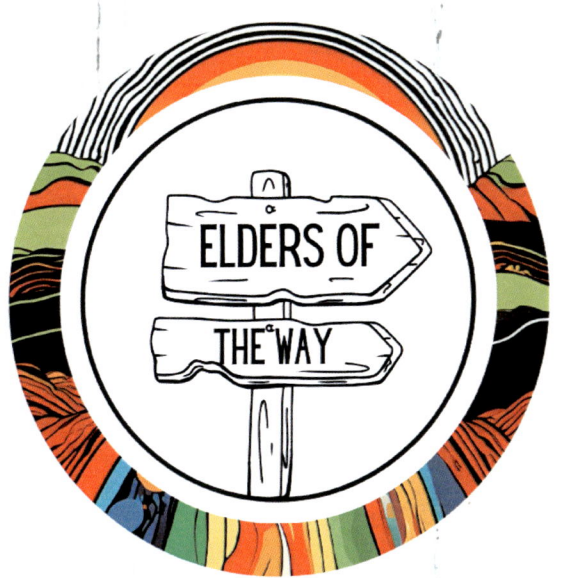

WELCOME

The Story

Harry and Annabelle

ELDERS OF THE WAY

Your ears will hear a voice behind you, saying, "This is the way, walk in it"

Isaiah 30:21

This is the story of an ancient dream reborn.

Through twists and turns it would travel from the Aboriginal village of Jubullum, to the Old City of Jerusalem, before planting itself in Hawaiʻi, a chain of islands found at the ends of the earth.

For a decade it would be called fellowship and family, in time they would call it *The Way*. This is how we got there, to the place where the pages flip themselves, as if the Author of Life truly was at work in the world around us.

It was 2012 when I landed after 10 years in the urban jungle of New York City, tracking an urge to connect with the elders of my homeland, a place of ancient peoples now known as Australia.

He was the great Poppy Harry Mundine Walker, Chief of the Wahlubal tribe, custodian of land and language, retired Reverend and legendary preacher they used to call *The Black Billy Graham*.

She was the amazing Aunty Annabelle, warrior of praise and prayer, the gospel singing, *corroboree* dancing, beloved wife, mum and nan, with a laugh that could leave you lying on the floor.

In time I would become their designated driver, healthcare liaison, anniversary planner, fish and chips coordinator, TV repairman, and singer of the old songs, among a host of other tasks. But my greatest would be learning what it meant to be their *godson*, as the narrow gate they led me through gave way to an ocean of responsibility.

They had encountered the Lord in the midst of revival on Pop's community in the 1950s and 60s, prayed over by the grandmothers and grandfathers, aunties and uncles who had wed the untold power of their traditions with the good news of a risen messiah. The messages and melodies they took to heart would carry them through a half century of trial and triumph, guiding them on the path to their own ministry, and Pop's historic ordination as an Aboriginal Reverend.

Faced with obstacles too many to manage, they would lay down their mission for a time, tending to health and family as they stepped into old age. But no matter the hill to climb or river to cross, whatever worries the world might throw at them, they would never lose sight of the One who gave them strength to do all things, and their relentless faith would come to transform lives once again.

They would emerge as my teachers and guides, stewards of a bridge to a past quickly fading,

Annabelle, Adam and Harry, 2012

warriors of the old ways praying for a willing ear to catch hold of those same messages and melodies in which they had found eternal freedom, the ones that seemed, and sounded, about as close to timeless as you could get.

Over a decade and more, their words would be a lamp unto my feet, and though I would end up halfway around the world, whatever the distance or cost, the Lord they trusted with all their might would faithfully reunite us, again and again.

And in the end, I would do my best to carry them with me, to the farthest reaches of the planet, where we prayed many more would take their tale to heart, and have no choice but to love them also, as our precious Pop and Ma, *Elders of The Way*.

THE CALLING

Part One

Aunty Annabelle Walker

TAKE ME TO AMERICA

And whatever you shall ask in my name, that will I do.

John 14:13

They were the first words out of her mouth.

We stood overlooking the Rocky River, a land of ancient chiefs and turtle divers, still home to the Wahlubal tribe after thousands of years.

New York had kept me captive for a decade before landing here, a dot on the map about as far from the Big City as one could get. Deep in the heartland of the Northern Rivers, over the range from Byron Bay, the most easterly point on the continent, this was a town so tiny, one blink and you could miss it.

To think how Jubullum would be woven into my life in the coming years was unimaginable, as we finished our meeting under the eucalyptus trees and an Aboriginal Aunty walked my way with an ear to ear smile, and an unforgettable request.

I want you to take me to America.

She loved those gospel preachers, she said, and had always wanted to see them in action. Why this indigenous elder from a country town in Australia would choose a *Jimmy Swaggert* pilgrimage over Paris or Tokyo as her first international trip had me puzzled, but the sparkle in her eyes revealed more than I needed to know. Though I couldn't make any promises on the travel front just yet, we pencilled in a day to catch up that week, and I hoped to be of help in some other way.

Winding back through the hills, I landed in Tabulam, where their beloved Rocky meets the Clarence River. This was a far cry from Times Square, those sky high billboards and the zig zag of yellow cabs, replaced by an old fashioned post office, pub and food co-op. Before I could ask around for help tracking down my new friend, an orange *Commodore* pulled up and there she was, jumping out of the drivers seat and happily accepting my invitation to lunch, and a *cuppa*.

While she ate her sandwich under the low hanging tin roof, I spoke of returning from America with a heart to help the elders of this my homeland, a simple thought, at least to me. Her reply, on the other hand, would shock me to a core I never knew I had, setting in motion events unfolding to this day.

"You're our angel!" she proclaimed, her hands raised to the ceiling. "God has sent you!"

Many years and countless *cuppas* later, I would begin to understand how much she had meant it, but at the time I was drifting from path to path, devoted to the quest, but failing to find whatever I thought I was

The Gospel Warrior at Church

looking for. So as her words washed over me, I felt like a spiritual fish out of water, coaxed from my comfort zone by the radiance with which her reply had been invested. And though I found myself at a loss for words, inside I had to admit that whatever *this* was, whoever *she* was, was unlike anything or anyone I had ever encountered.

Looking back I would recall her proclamation as the Author of Days turning the page on my life as a wandering soul, calling me to serve this Aunty and her husband, and in doing so, learning to serve the will of the Almighty, who in these words of hers, had brought us together. Our friendship would blossom as the months rolled by, and soon we would take our first ride together, my hands at the wheel as we set our sights for the coast, turning onto the old *Bruxner Highway* on the way out of Tabulam.

At the Rocky River, 2015

"Can I pray for our journey?" she had asked, and I imagined her head bowed, palms pressed together, like the people I'd seen on TV over the years, good little boys and girls saying their bedtime prayer, a group of nuns blessing their soup and bread, neatly-dressed families in long wooden pews, reciting *Hallowed Be Thy Name* in unison.

"Lord, I command your angels go before us!" Aunty roared, her hands held high. "Clear the road of all animals and obstacles!" she spoke with a power that seemed to extend yards in front of us, like a supernatural barrier of protection. "And give us a safe journey and mercy, in *Jesus'* name!"

In an instant, hurtling down the highway at 100km an hour, everything I thought I knew about prayer had changed, and my mind adjusted to a reality in which my new friend might just be the mightiest of spiritual warriors I had ever met. A window to faith had been cracked by this woman I had barely met, but clearly admired, my misperceptions about spiritual power cast aside by a prayer that seemed to lift the car off the road. Whatever truth was behind this display, I sensed it was something embedded in her bones, a living, breathing reality she walked and talked out every day, something a lifetime of prayers prayed and answered would leave no doubt.

And no matter how hard it was to process at first, or how complex the conversations with those I knew and loved might become, despite everything the world had told me to think, here was a mountainous truth appearing on the horizon of this path I had pushed away every time a sign had presented itself. In time I would see it revealed in hearts healed and lives transformed, in scenes I couldn't have written, and a story I wouldn't have dreamed of dreaming. But where I saw it most, was in the unfolding miracle that was this Aunty living in the Lord's strength through trial upon trial, praying ceaselessly, whether for the ride before us, or for the great journeys all must take in life and loss.

Her words and ways would embed themselves in my memory, shining a flame in the darkest of times, the echo of her voice reminding me that the Lord would always *make a way out of no way*. And no matter the journey to come, in one way or another, I would take this beloved Aunty to America, even if it meant her traveling in the hearts and minds, the songs and stories of those who, like me, would come to know her affectionately, as *Ma*.

Poppy Harry Mundine Walker

TWO BOOMERANGS AND A CROSS

*And he has committed to us
the message of reconciliation.*

2 Corinthians 5:19

He was a bridge between worlds.

The last boy born before the tribe was moved onto the mission in the 1940s, raised in the ways and words of his Wahlubal ancestors. The father of eight working late in the asbestos mine, shocked to hear a voice from above telling him to lay down his shovel and become a preacher.

"But I don't like people!" he had shouted back, before obeying the call and going on to become one of the most beloved shepherds of his generation.

He had seen old fashioned revival breathe life into his community, before the empty promise of progress clutched it from the hands of those walking in the old people's footsteps. And yet, the waves of change, their peaks and valleys, would never rock his trust in the Constant, Reliable, Unchanging One.

It was my first ride alone with the old fella, the man introduced to me as Poppy Harry, and we watched the ancient green hills he knew so well pass us by. Here and there he would share a story about the sights we were seeing, but mostly we sat in a gentle silence that grew more comfortable as the hours passed. Arriving at our destination, an Aboriginal church up the coast in *Fingal* that was celebrating its 100th anniversary, we parked the car and stepped into the tent that had been raised for the occasion.

The morning service was in full swing, and I looked around to see dozens of smiling faces, both black and white, welcoming us with a warmth that took me by surprise. The truth was, I had always felt a bit uncomfortable in church settings, but I had to admit there was something special about this place, and these people. And though I knew little to nothing about church life in general, it seemed natural to be moved by the rich history of this ministry, one that had survived so many seasons, keeping the doors open long enough for the two of us to walk through them today, a full century after the first spiritual stone had been laid.

As the songs came to an end and the Pastor stepped to the pulpit, my eyes were struck by the symbols placed squarely at its center, a hand crafted combination I had never seen before.

Two boomerangs and a cross.

This was a convergence of culture and spirit, the ancient ones of Australia coming face to face with a holy preacher and teacher from Galilee who, having overcome death two millennia ago, was still transforming lives in a country church halfway

Welcome to Church by the Reverend

around the planet. If these seemingly divergent pathways had been reconciled here in this tent, and in the hearts of those gathered in song and prayer, it seemed they had found a way to span this gap I had thought of as beyond bridging, a meeting place with the power to unite traditions, and peoples.

I thought about Poppy Harry, the Chief who took me to church, and how he himself was a bridge between worlds. This was a man who loved the ancient ways of his people, and *The Way* of his Lord, a man upon whose legacy many more might one day cross that sea of uncertainty between old and new, black and white, settled and settler, the things we were told existed to separate us, only to find there exists a Rock of Ages upon which we all can stand, an Everlasting One through whom all people, and all things, can and will be reconciled.

Welcome to Country by the Chief

Over a lunch of cold cuts and salad in the aging wooden hall nearby, I watched Poppy Harry laugh with his friends, their joy at reuniting after months or years filling the room with a peace that would soften the hardest of hearts. The scene would repeat itself in the seasons to come, my role as driver and helper introducing me to the faithful across the region. But despite their difference in ancestry or upbringing, whether from a town of a hundred, or a city of a million, the people I met seemed woven into a tapestry no human hand could thread, a force no eyes could see, yet one made crystal clear in the moving of this Spirit I would hear them sing about.

Come Holy Spirit I need thee
Come Sweet Spirit I pray
Come in your strength and your power
Come in your own gentle way

The more I got to know Poppy Harry and Aunty Annabelle, the more I heard the travel prayers and steered the wheel to church, I would be drawn to know what drove them to follow this thing called *The Way,* to unravel the depth at its core, a message and a man with the power to speak life to every human heart. They were the living remnants of an indigenous-led revival, one that had inspired a generation of preachers and teachers to call their own. Ever since, they had walked a ministry marathon, tending to their flocks and allowing the Lord to establish their steps, even if they edged against the norms of society. And though their eyes might see shades of skin, their ears might hear an accent from a land unlike their own, to them, everyone was family in the family of God, a brother, a sister, a beloved for all time.

In a world crying out for reconciliation, they were living it out in spirit, and in practice. In an age where indigenous culture and the church seemed at odds, they had found a path to redemption that sought honor for all sides. When we had started the journey that morning, I would have been happy to deliver *The Chief* here and home without any major mishaps. A decade later, I would remember it as the first in a long line of adventures that would increasingly take on a life of their own, with a route only He who sees all things would even consider mapping. But even without the benefit of hindsight, as we drove away that day, I knew that wherever the destination, if the old fella was headed there, it was the way I wanted to follow, whether he was guiding us as the one they named *The Reverend*, or as the man we would come to know lovingly, as *Pop*.

With The Godson, 2022

THIS FAMILY WAS FOREVER

The Spirit you received brought about your adoption to sonship.

Romans 8:15

A Roman adoption was for keeps.

When a favored servant was brought into the family, made a son and citizen of the empire, it was a legally binding process that couldn't be revoked.

This family was forever.

And so it was that the Apostle Paul described the adoption of a heart restored to relationship with the Everlasting Father, keys to the Kingdom in hand, slave to a fearful world no more.

Now if we are children, then we are heirs.

In time I would learn how one goes about accessing this divine inheritance, as well as the sacrifice it took to pay off our debts that we might be granted our freedom. But first I would be called to study the science of *sonship* under the wings of two elders who had already learned these lessons of a lifetime, the ones who would rear me lovingly on *The Way*.

It all changed when they appeared out of nowhere, sitting by the roadside in Casino, the country town over the hills from Jubullum. The stars were out and the streets were empty as I drove back into range, anxious to check on my bank balance.

From head to toe, the relief struck like gold, as I saw the payment sitting in my account, and I turned onto Barker Street, keen to grab a feed and fill up the tank before heading home for the coast. Searching for an open restaurant, I saw two silhouettes on a bench up ahead, and though I was unlikely to know anyone here, two hours inland from my home, as they came into view it seemed I had indeed made their acquaintance before.

Poppy Harry and Aunty Annabelle.

I pulled over and jumped out, their faces lit with surprise to see me driving around these streets at an hour like this. But when I asked how they were, Aunty's face grew strained as she told me about their car registration due in a few days, a bill beyond their means, and one if gone unpaid would make the trip to and from town a challenge every time.

"You won't believe this," I said, without hesitation. "I just got paid for the first time in months."

We were still getting to know each other, and though they could have tried to talk me out of it, my quick departure didn't give them a chance.

"Wait here and I'll go get you the cash," I waved as I zipped around to the ATM, returning a few minutes

The 70th Birthday in Tabulam, 2013

later to hand Poppy Harry the bank notes that would lift their burden. They praised God and sat me down on the bench in between them, praying for me for the very first time, giving thanks *for this their son* who had appeared in the dark to provide for their needs.

Our connection would deepen in the months that followed, and being in service, being a *son*, whatever that entailed, would quickly emerge as a pillar of purpose in my life, my affection for them growing steadily beyond that of a friend, or helper. Aunty would solidify the bond further while celebrating her 70th birthday at a barbecue and home spun gospel rally in the park at Tabulam. Calling Harry, their sons and daughters, grandkids and all the *jarjums* up on stage for a family photo, she would summon me over the loudspeaker, her voice hollering with an invitation to remember.

By the Rocky River, 2013

"Come on Adam, you're part of the family now!"

The growing ties between us had become difficult to define, until a friend's story with familiar undertones prompted me to ask Pop and Ma if they would be my *godparents*, a request they happily accepted. Not only had they worked to weave the Lord into my life in a way I never knew I needed, I hadn't grown up with godparents, and it seemed to fill as much a familial role, as it did a spiritual one.

"The Godson," Pop would introduce me to friends and family, pointing in my direction.

It would take years to reveal the responsibility attached to the role, but something present from the beginning was a mutual gratitude for whatever the

Lord was doing, a fact made clear the next time I saw Aunty on stage, this time holding her own under the brights lights of a festival called to celebrate the indigenous tribes of the region.

"I'm proud to be an Aboriginal woman!" she exclaimed, to a packed house of many colors. After thanking God for being there and meeting so many nice people, she turned to me at the side of the stage.

"And I thank God for my godson Adam," she told the audience. "I never thought I'd have a white son!"

She cracked herself up, her raucous laughter rousing the room to join in, making it a moment I would never forget, though one I would reflect upon with great care as I tried to fathom what it would take to hold up my end of the bargain. It wouldn't always be easy, and I would fail to live up to my own expectations many a time, but what mattered most was the sprouting of our connection seemed to stem from God's own adoption of the broken and weary, a bonding in the spirit that could never be undone.

For no matter how it might be described, or seen from a distance, through the many ups and downs, the lessons and the learnings, wherever the seasons of life might take us, she would be my Ma, he would be my Pop, and though coming from worlds apart, despite our differences in culture and the color of our skin, no matter what, praise God, I would be their son.

jarjums
kids

The Old Church at Jubullum

STANDING ON HOLY GROUND

*And they shall rebuild the old ruins,
they shall raise up the former desolations.*

Isaiah 61:4 NKJV

This is where the old people had prayed.

At first glance it looked like another empty lot on the mission, but this grassy field meant more than most could imagine, and as we got out of the car, Pop walked ahead onto the site where their beloved community church once stood.

He and Ma's 50th wedding anniversary was around the corner, and when I offered to plan a celebration to fit the occasion, he told me of a long held wish that would bring them joy like no other.

To hold church here once again.

As we came to the place where the building had stood proudly before losing its battle with time, we could see the stone foundations still in the ground, partially hidden under grass growing wildly where this village had once gathered to sing and pray.

The powers that be had promised to build a new one, Pop said, but never had, and he spoke of it as the *lighthouse* going out in their community, and never coming back on. Listening to the longing in his voice, I strained to imagine the glory that was once revealed here, and knew we had to do whatever we could to help them rebuild, if only for a day.

The anniversary arrived and we busied ourselves raising a pair of store bought tents on top of the old foundations, piecing a pop-up sanctuary together, one numbered pole at a time. As we worked we watched the cars arrive from near and far, neighbors from around the bend, elders from across the region, church friends old and new. Pastor Bruce Walker, Pop's cousin and childhood adventure buddy, arrived with his keyboard in tow, setting up with his band of friends and family. Knowing how much this site must have meant to him also, I had a poster of the old church framed for Pop to gift him, his fellow keeper of the old time memories.

After opening with prayer and worship, the elders shared stories of the place we had gathered, and what a gift it was for them to be back there. And then, lifting their voices mightily, they sang one of their favorites, a chorus so perfect you could have thought it was written for the soil beneath our feet.

We are standing on holy ground

It had taken years of dreaming, but on this sunny summer morning, the old church at Jubullum was humming once more, and a new generation was catching a glimpse of God's love poured out in this

A Pop Up Sanctuary on the Old Foundations, 2016

place. To think of Pop and Ma and Pastor Bruce standing here in the 1960s, linking arms with their brothers and sisters, cousins and colleagues in Christ, praying in one accord, having no idea that some day in the distant future we would be here helping them remember the best of those days.

And I know there are angels all around

What would it take to rekindle the fire of that era, to know what a church on the mission could mean to the offspring of old, a piece of them surely aching for more than modernity had to offer. Today may have made Pop and Ma's anniversary wish come true, but the real dream was wishing it would go on forever, like in the olden days when the next church rally was always just around the corner of the calendar.

Pop and Ma on their 50th Wedding Anniversary, 2016

After the service, we headed up the road for lunch and cake in the hall, before making our way back to the pop-up site, where the word on the street was the elders were planning their own afternoon service. We arrived to a church that had quickly taken flight, old time country gospel and full-throated testimony blasting through Pastor Alfie's tried and true speakers and into the surrounding homes, families gathered on porches to take in the echoes of worship that had been so common long ago.

The microphone passed hand to hand, visitors invited to share a song, a prayer, or a story of God's goodness. I had never seen church done with this much openness and laughter, everyone welcomed to participate in some way, as if we had stumbled back in time and the Lord was revealing a way of gathering that had been lost to the modern world.

Looking around, I noticed that aside from the two of us, we were now at an all-Aboriginal gathering, on the very site where an all-Aboriginal church had housed revival some six decades prior. This was a service that seemed to emerge from the very dust underneath our feet, prayed to life by the children and grandchildren of those who had first revealed *The Way* in this place. And here we were, foreigners welcomed as family, seeing up close the miracle of an old fella's vision made vibrantly real.

I fell to my knees, my hands on the foundations of the building that had brought so many into the presence of God in times past. And for the first time since I could remember, I wept, bearing witness to this rare and raw gathering of the saints, given even the tiniest taste of what it might have been like when the people of old praised the One who could raise up any desolation. And to be used as I had, hearing the call of Pop's heart and trusting in the rest, content that my tiny role had played its part in making their 50th anniversary one to remember.

Ma's voice fished me back from what had felt like an eternity, and I jumped up to fetch her a drink, returning to my duties in service to these beloved elders on their special day. Years later, I would recall that minute of awe and brokenness, knowing it alone would have made a decade of service and sacrifice worth every penny. In time we would make plans to build a new church in Jubullum, but for today this one had done just fine, for the ground underneath it was holy, and those gathered were over the ***gibam*** to be there, as the sun set and their voices rose as one, praising the Lord like old.

gibam
moon

Baptisms in the Rocky River, 1950s

SHALL WE GATHER AT THE RIVER

*Then the angel showed me the river of
the water of life, as clear as crystal.*

Revelation 22:1

This was their Jordan River.

At Pop's command, we pulled our cars off the old dirt road, glancing over the hills that he knew like the back of his hand.

Below us was the Rocky, a waterway central to Wahlubal life for thousands of years, where the young descendants of the Original Peoples still cooled off in summer, diving for short-necked turtles, a local delicacy.

But it was another chapter in the Rocky's rich history that had brought us to its banks today. In the 1950s, revival had come to the village of Jubullum, young and old drawn to the saving power of the gospel.

While we might give God an hour on Sunday morning, or often none at all, these faith-filled and fired-up warriors of yesteryear would sometimes meet three times a day, *every day of the week.*

Pop had told us of the crowds who came from all over, including preachers from over the seas, called to sing the old songs, to hear the old sermons, and to be baptized in the river. And now here we were, standing on the site where his uncles and aunties, family and friends had committed their hearts to the Lord, emerging from the ancient waters to breathe their first breath of life as a new creation.

We placed our folding chairs in a half circle and listened to the stories of a bygone era, made all the more real by the aged color photos Pop had brought to show us, one of which he claimed to be hiding in as a teenager across the bank of the river. As we prayed for their community, and for the heart of revival to return to its midst, I felt a seed of sadness that a history so rich might be lost to time, barely kept alive in the memories of an aging handful who would soon go home to be with their Savior.

Six years later, I would sit quietly at the kitchen table with the old fella, giving him time to think. We had spent the week at home, just the two of us, devoting many an hour to tracking down his favorite old hymns. His face lit up when he heard the resulting playlist, the country gospel hits of the 1960s and 70s drawing out stories from the long life he and Annabelle had led. But hearing them had also sparked a longing for more, hymns from another time that could heal the heart with a tender verse, or open the gates of heaven with a tent-raising chorus.

"I'm trying to remember the old songs," he said in a hushed tone, his eyes closed firmly. "The ones the old people used to sing."

At the Rocky River, 2015

I imagined the ears of a young Harry hearing those voices of decades long gone, his 80 year old self willing him back to those beloved times.

"Mmm… gather at the river… shall we gather at the river," he said, nodding slowly.

We flipped through a few versions on YouTube, the old fella amazed at what you could find with this little phone of mine. He pointed out the version he liked the best, and I picked up the chords on the guitar, giving us a chance to sing it ourselves.

Yes! We'll gather at the river
The beautiful, beautiful river
Gather with the saints at the river
That flows by the throne of God

Overlooking the Rocky River, 1950s

Pop clapped along and cheered as the song came back to life before him, an old church classic with wings to carry him back to the way things used to be, when he'd heard it for the first time.

"Make sure you really get the *Yes!*" he laughed. "The old people would really cry out on that one!"

The next time I saw that vintage color photo of the baptisms in the river, remembering the time he took us up there to pray, my mind longed for a sample of what it might have sounded like in an old revival meeting on the mission in the 1950s. I imagined the elders calling the service to a close with an invitation for all gathered to join them up river, where new believers would arise from the Rocky, born again in the spirit of the living God.

And I knew, as impossible a task as it might seem, if we could capture even a hint of that sound, this river that had flooded the hearts of the old people, the one that had carried Pop and Ma from shore to shore, would continue its flow into the future, quenching the spiritual thirst of seekers near and far.

For soon this song, and the others in its wake, would carve a melodic trail of their own, building bridges from church to church, and across the seas. And as they did, what would flow was the testimony of these two saints, and a story of revival that sprung from the banks of an ancient river where souls had come in search of the very spring of life.

Yes! We'll gather at the river
The beautiful, beautiful river
Gather with the saints at the river
That flows by the throne of God

As the crowds had gathered long ago, and we had done so that day, we prayed that the saints might return to the Rocky, crying out a mighty *Yes!* as we gather to celebrate another generation of seekers finding hope in the living waters of the One who makes all things new. Whether it took weeks, months or a decade to fulfill, it was a dream we would carry to the ends of the earth and back if need be, for the mighty river that flowed by the throne of God had wound its way here, and it was a well the elders had dug so deep, it would never ever run dry.

Blazing the Holy Trail

CALL THEM OUT OF THE WORLD

And this is the testimony: God has given us eternal life, and this life is in his Son.

1 John 5:11

They'd been called from across the globe.

120 young leaders, eager with anticipation, gathered for the opening day of a summer program sending them onto the streets of our coastal town, caring for those in need, and sharing the good news of a Lord who loves, and saves.

The organizer came to the mic and welcomed the packed room, before introducing some very special guests who had been invited to bless their mission.

Pop and Ma.

The three of us were finding a rhythm when called to visit a church, speak at a school, or attend a festival across the region. Pop would welcome the crowd in Wahlubal, translating into English that he was thanking the Lord and asking Him to bless all those gathered. Sometimes he would share a short sermon, or a story of the olden days, before turning to introduce his beloved Annabelle.

"This… is my wife," he said, almost with a wink in his spirit, knowing the fun that might be in store as she stepped into the spotlight.

"Good morning," Annabelle began, no more than a few responding politely.

"I can't hear you!" she shouted, as if announcing the fighters at a heavyweight boxing match.

"Good morning!!!" the crowd erupted as one, instantly wrapped around her little finger.

Whatever the occasion, Ma would do all she could to release the fire of heaven, praising God and testifying to His transformative power in her life, the blessing He had been for her family and community. It was a sight to behold, the ripple effects of her salvation half a century ago still setting waves in motion for those lucky enough to hear her speak.

"Before I became a Christian I was a bad person," she would say, to a few uncertain looks. "I was a fighter and a drinker and all that, you wouldn't have wanted to know me back then."

"But one day I was in the back of the old church on the mission," her tone catching stride. "And I heard a voice telling me to go down the front."

"I didn't want to be a Christian!" she exclaimed, her laughter putting the crowd at ease. "But the next thing I knew I was up the front, and the old people were all around me praying, and I felt this *POW—ER* come upon me!"

At Pastor Alfie and Irene's Church, Casino, 2019

Her raised hand moved slowly down the front of her body as she spoke, illustrating the encounter that had changed her life for good. And just like that, the presence would blanket her again, as if it was the hand of the Lord descending through the decades, here to offer that same power to anyone else who might be ready to receive it.

"And I just thank God cause I felt the miracle going through me when the elders prayed for me in that church that night," she continues, still moved by the memory. "God changed me, I felt all the hatred leave, and I was a completely new person."

"The best gift you could ever receive is salvation," she would say. "And I praise God every day for saving me, changing me, and making me into who he wanted me to be."

Singing the Old Songs with Ma, 2018

After 50 years of sharing it, hers was a testimony for all time, and here was a new generation gathered from near and far, witnesses to the boundless power attached to its telling. After coming to a close, Ma would call on me to sing a chorus, and I strummed my guitar, starting us off with the opening line to one of her favorites.

He is our peace, he has broken down every wall

Ma's was a voice that could lift up the weariest of hearts and break down the mightiest of strongholds, a soaring set of tones on a mission to pull the richness of the past into a moment we didn't know we had been waiting for.

So cast your cares on him, cause he cares for you

The words she sang seemed embedded in the fabric of her life story, embodied in the poise with which she carried herself, emboldened by the walking, talking piece of evidence that she was, proof that the saving power of the gospel could melt the resistance of a hardened mind, lighting this flame in the human heart with fuel to burn for eternity.

The gathering moved to a close and all who wanted to be blessed by Pop and Ma were invited to come forward, dozens of bright young faces lining up before us. One by one, these beloved elders laid hands on the next generation of saints, asking God to *call them out of the world*, that many might be touched and saved through their ministries. It had been countless seasons since they'd had an opportunity like this, to speak into the lives of an army of future leaders, many of whom would remember this day, and these two servants of the Lord, for the rest of their lives. What a blessing it was for both giver and given, a legacy of faith honored by eager hearts, open to receiving the tales and teachings of those who had blazed the holy trail before them.

This was the calling the elders had followed, the one Pop and Ma were extending to us. But how many more were out there, walking through life without having heard the old girl sing, or the old fella preach, without feeling the power of a 50 year old testimony, or seeing a Chief bridge the worlds of culture and faith? What Pop and Ma needed was a way to pass on that which they had stewarded with such care, for so long. How that would come about, and who might be tasked with such a responsibility, would soon come like a fire to consume my world.

Teach me, Lord, the way of your decrees, that I may follow it to the end.

Psalm 119:33

THE TORCH

Part Two

The Day Before Surgery, 2016

THIS LIFE GIVING GIFT

*Show me your ways, Lord,
teach me your paths.*

Psalm 25:4

Our VIP was a *Very Important Patient*.

It was cancer, the surgeon had said, and I dropped everything to care for Pop through his operation and recovery. Now the seconds seemed to count themselves as we waited on edge for an update.

A friendly nurse approached with the news we needed to hear, that he was safely recuperating in the *Intensive Care Unit*, and I was welcome to go in and see him, having been listed as his next-of-kin.

He would likely be asleep for the rest of the night, I was told, as we passed machine after machine, beeping to the beats of life. But when we approached his quarters, and the nurse pulled the curtain to the side, this *Very Important Patient* was very much awake, eyeing us attentively.

"That's strange," she said, surprised to see him so alert. "He's the Chief," I replied, relieved beyond measure to see the old fella on the other side.

"Is there anything I can do for you Pop?" I asked, as he closed his eyes to consider my offer.

"Isaiah 61," he responded quietly, and I sat by the side of his bed, opening the hand-sized Bible he had dedicated to me just the day before.

The Spirit of the Lord GOD is upon me

"Mmmm," he said when I finished, pausing again to think. "Psalm 27."

The Lord is my light and my salvation

A few more of his favorites would follow, before he called me in closer, speaking in Wahlubal.

Woogar-gu ngai gala
Wooreh ee-em-bee

"Show me your ways, that I might follow you," Pop translated, granting me a few tries at the original, happy to hear his language spoken back to him. Barely on the other side of a life saving surgery, he seemed consciously aware of making the most of this moment, as if awakened on a mission to share the things he had been dreaming of.

Knowing what a gift this time might become would take years to unwrap in its entirety, but for now one thing was clear, I was here to listen, and to learn. Resting in the ward the next morning, his darling Annabelle by his side, Pop began to translate one of their favorite old hymns into Wahlubal, writing out the lyrics by hand in my new golden notebook.

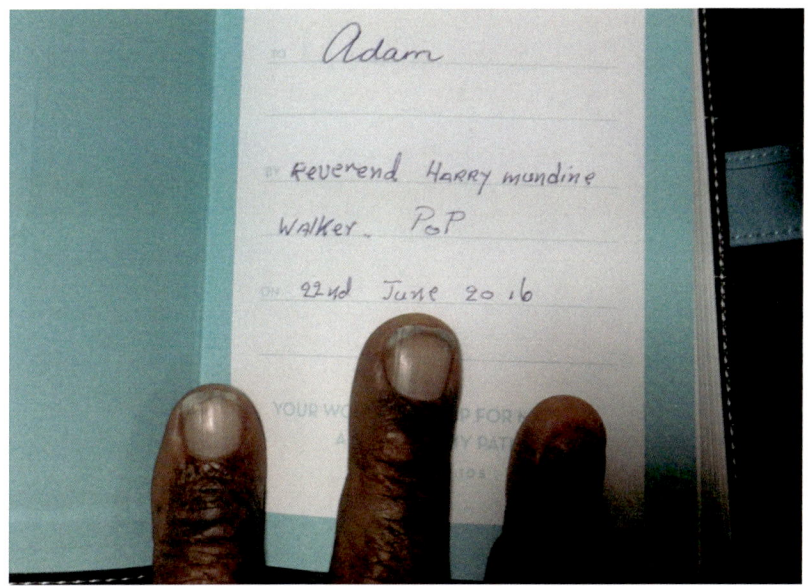

The Newly Dedicated Bible, 2016

Marmung-u yogombeh wuluni
Woggai dulong whernbi

For God has not given to us
A spirit of fear

Catching the melody from Ma, I strummed some chords as our voices filled the ward with the lyrics sung in English *and* Wahlubal, the old fella overjoyed to hear it brought to life at such a time as this.

Mugga muggi wernbi
Boogle wernbi
Mindle wernbi

But of power
And of love
And of sound mind

Godfather and Godson, 2017

For the rest of his stay, I barely left Pop's side, talking with doctors and nurses, taking phone calls from the family, and filling the golden notebook with songs, scripture and photos illustrating the extraordinary life that he, praise God, was still living out. On the day of his discharge, Pop took the notebook in his hands, flipping through page after page, his eyes brightening with every turn.

"Gee hey," he said. "I want one!"

While we had prayed he would survive this storm, Pop's undying faith had led him not just to the other side, but to a mountaintop from where he could see the Lord using this challenge to do a good work through us. The seeds he planted through those long days and nights seemed to grow with every season, especially when my own clouds of life rolled in.

Cause even in the valley of the shadow of death, one could always ask the Lord to *show us His ways, that we might follow Him*, a teaching Pop had shared in the wake of a second chance, an old fella back from the brink, opening his eyes to find this servant of his also had ears to hear. His confidence in the face of adversity was beyond explanation, until he made clear that it came from casting your cares on the One who conquered death itself.

A year later, Pop would hold the microphone at my birthday, *fit as a fiddle* and cancer free, reflecting on what had taken place during that time.

"When I went up to Brisbane hospital to get a liver operation, Adam came every morning at seven o'clock, sat down by my bedside, and he stayed there all day until it was time for the visiting hours at night," he recalled, reminding me of the ebbs and flows of a ward that had started to feel like home. "And you know, that really *really* blessed me, the things he did, the things he done, how he comforted me, and helped me on the road to recovery."

"It was there that I taught him some of the songs in language, and I'm a bit jealous now," he paused, prompting a few sideways glances in the crowd. "Because he sings them better than I do!"

The room roared with laughter, the uncertainty of those long days and nights replaced by a window into the wonder-working ways of the One who shines His light into the darkest of times, a heavenly touch that could turn a life threatening illness into *this life giving gift*, for godfather and godson.

Pop in the Fields at Jubullum, 2019

SHEEP FOR THE SHEPHERD

Let me inherit a double portion of your spirit.

2 Kings 2:9

The teachings were not of this world.

They lit hearts on fire, brought healing and redemption, and have, for two thousand years since, opened the gates to the temple of the Almighty.

But in the span of a single generation, the saving power of the gospel had been drowned out by a million and one messages pouring in from all sides. With a menu of paths to pick from, a hundred channels to flick through, and a thousand friends to please with every post, instant rewards had edged out the pursuit of eternal peace.

So here was Pop, a mighty man of God, anointed preacher and thoughtful teacher, forever willing and able to share the mysteries of the Kingdom, his knowledge sorely needed if we were to turn the tide in the quest for weary souls. And yet, what was missing were *sheep for the shepherd*, fertile fields of the heart and mind in which to sow these seeds of wisdom, gathered from a lifetime of good learning.

It felt like the sun was rising in my chest as I let out a deep *A—MEN,* the kind that Pop had shaken into my bones after a month at his side, caring for his every need. I had learned to lean into this new sensation while sharing a tiny room with the old fella, each of us on our own twin sized bed, discovering how powerful a single word can be, when your whole body knows how to speak it.

"If you listen to much of what I talk about, it could be a sign for you," Pop had said. Being in close proximity, day and night, had given us a rare amount of one-on-one quiet time, and it seemed the most important teachings were imparted in the midst of those moments, with our without words.

"Maybe because so far you're listening and you're doing a lot of the work that we talk about, that we read about, you're listening, you see?" Pop continued. "Remember what Proverbs was telling us, it says: My son bind these things around your neck, around your fingers, listen to what I'm saying, that's what He's saying. Don't forget 'em. Don't turn this way, that way, but just look ahead."

Over the years, Pop had offered snippets of wisdom here and there, but I was now being prompted to take stock of the role someone in my shoes might have in receiving them. What that meant in the long run was beyond me at the time, and I would have valleys to cross in life before it had sunk in on the level it deserved. The old fella, on the other hand, was always one step ahead, seeing the potential in the process taking place, forever on the lookout for a way to catch my attention.

Driving back from Old America, Tabulam, 2018

"What's that Scripture about Elijah and Elisha?" he had asked, and I leafed through my Bible until I came to 1 Kings.

Then he set out to follow Elijah and became his servant

Without blinking, I had said *Yes* to the call to care for him through an immense trial, and the experience, though challenging in so many ways, had served as a mighty mutual blessing. Pop had gotten the coordinator and companion he needed to see the journey through, but he had found a student as well as a servant, hearing him when he says *to listen is to learn, and to learn is to listen.*

I had heard the Old Testament stories of Elijah, being miraculously sustained by God, calling *down* the fire of heaven to call *out* the false prophets of the age.

Calling a New Generation of Disciples, 2017

He had found his student of choice plowing a field, placing his cloak over him in an act that would signify the call to be his disciple. This man named Elisha would be his apprentice, witnessing many miracles and being positioned to receive the generational blessing of his teacher. His final request of the famous prophet, whose legendary footsteps he was following, was significant enough to be recorded in the history books.

Let me inherit a double portion of your spirit

When poor health had sidelined Pop's ministry work, he had lost his flock, his best chance at passing on a lifetime of experience. The more I understood the significance of who he was, and what he might be carrying, the more I saw how fragile the thread of teaching between generations had become. There were a million reasons why the links in the chain were eroding, and in time we would work to restore as many of them as we could, but for now the only thing to do was say *Yes* to whatever was unfolding.

The spirit of Elijah is resting on Elisha

Through prayer and prophecy, by the laying on of hands, from the calling of a fisherman, to the draping of a cloak, the anointing of a disciple was a much-storied tradition. But history aside, for us in the here and now, at war with a world determined to cut the ancient thread connecting us to *The Way, The Truth and The Life*, any opportunity to listen and to learn from those who paved the path before us was the gift of a lifetime, and beyond.

In being a servant to Pop, he had taught me to lay down the longings of my mind, that I might have room to serve the One who knows the desires of the heart. In being his student, I saw him pointing to the teacher of teachers, praying we too might become disciples of the Master, the One through whom the insights of the ages were made accessible to people of every land and language.

As much as I had been committed to the task at hand, this was a mission for all who heard the call to sit at the feet of our elders, to witness the wisdom of old at work in the world, to match the fearless faith they reveal in their prayers, the ones crying out for the gospel to sweep across the land, that the madness of modern life might be washed away by an ocean of hearts keeping to the beat of A-MEN.

Harry Walker of Yesteryear

THE SOURCE OF OUR SUPPLY

It is He who made us, and we are His.

Psalm 100:3

Two words that could change everything.

The sun shone into the garage in Jubullum, as I scanned the verses the old fella had requested I read aloud, a morning Psalm to bless our trip into town.

Shout for joy to the Lord, all the earth
Worship the Lord with gladness

"Did you catch those two words?" Pop had asked.

Know that the Lord is God
It is He who made us, and we are His

Still grasping for an answer, I shook my head.

"See those words," Pop replied. "*He* and *His*."

Landing in a tiny Aboriginal village after a decade in New York City, I often felt how foreign I was to this place, a land stewarded by the wisdom of the elders, one of whom was patiently trying to unscramble my mind from the matrix of modernity.

So when Pop asked what two words stood out for me in Psalm 100, I searched for the most compelling, something to unlock the spiritual mystery he seemed poised to present. But like so much of the old fella's teaching, it was far more simple than my Big City brain could decipher, despite his best attempts at rewiring my thought process while he was deep in recovery from a life saving operation.

"The world we're living in has many sorts of ways," he had prayed late one evening. "But the oil that you give us is the greatest oil of all, and you pour it out upon us with your own hands, you touch us with it, *with your own hands*." He paused, seeming to sense an unseen guest, before continuing in language.

Marmung woodja ngallingnee
Woogar-gu muggi wernbi gungali

"Oil, oil, oil," he whispered, his words dripping with delight. "See how simple things can get."

Reminiscing about the church of times past, he would rub his thumb and fingers together slowly, telling us when the old people preached, you could really *feel* it. Their words were tied to the earth beneath our feet, he said, easy to understand, but powerful as could be. The ones he remembered from the early days were sadly long gone, but they had sowed their seeds into the man sitting before me, and the way he talked and taught about God seemed to shine from the very heart of yesteryear.

Heavenly sunshine, heavenly sunshine
Flooding my soul with glory divine

Heavenly Sunshine at Home

"A heavenly sunshine that covers you, protects you," he would say. "And he shines that sunshine on you because that's His, He created it, He gave it to us, He said *'There you go, you can use it.'*"

This was a man who was both Chief and Reverend, yet one who knew the humble words of the heart had the best chance at keeping a soul on the path of righteousness. "It's all in Proverbs 1 to 6," he told me once, the keeper of an ancient language, a lifelong teacher of the gospel, a man of native wisdom and biblical education, pointing to a handful of King Solomon's sayings as the secret to a life well lived. To lean not on our own understanding, to fall not into fear for how we might provide, was simply trusting in a God who is faithful and just, the giver of all gifts, *the source of our supply.*

A Wise Man of Simple Ways, 2017

Woondeleh. Ngarr. Gunghah.

To *stop, look* and *listen* was the key, Pop had said, age old skills that had gone *walkabout* in the fast paced lives the young ones were living. I had been one of those lost in the sea of screens screaming *look here, look there,* only to wash up at the feet of an old fella calling me to see what I couldn't have before.

"You see," said Pop, pointing at the Bible in my hands, still open to Psalm 100.

"*He* made us, we are *His* people."

I listened intently, a skill I was slowly picking up from my time with him, years of waiting on the edge of my seat, granting him the space worthy of his eldership. Only then did the words strike their intended chord, the depth of who *He* is, the Maker of all things, heaven, earth and in between, the One who spoke galaxies, oceans and mountains into being, was the same *He* who found it in *His* heart to paint us into the masterpiece of *His* making. And just as the birds of Creation find nurture under the Creator's wings, our peace would rest in our role as heirs to the Everlasting Father, adopted into *His* family, at home in *His* arms, now and forevermore.

This was the message Pop was sharing in the simplest of ways, for when we know who *He* is, we know who *we* are, prodigal sons and daughters restored to a living, loving God, not some being in the farthest reaches of the universe, or beyond, but in the most present and personal of ways, *His* voice speaking to the depths of the heart, with words only *He* knows how to whisper.

For the Lord is good and his love endures forever
His faithfulness continues through all generations

Many seasons had turned since the Father sent his Son to overcome the world, that we might be freed from its chains of ever growing complexity. It had been many more since a short Psalm calling us to shout for joy had been penned, the author unaware of the generational impact it would have. For here we were, thousands of years in the future, discipled by a wise man of simple ways, a Chief who taught us by surrendering any claims to mastery, other than knowing how to point to the One who so delights in His Creation, that the minds of those He has made might be reached and renewed, by two of the most humble words in human history.

The Chief's Golden Notebook

LEAVING A LEGACY OF GOLD

Write them on the tablet of your heart.

Proverbs 3:3

It was a notebook fit for a Chief.

Pop had held mine in his hands while resting in the hospital, the songs and teachings he shared after surgery, captured with care on page after page.

Now I was honoring his request for one to call his own, knowing my only real option was to mightily outshine the original. So, as I walked the aisles of the office superstore, hunting for something that looked like a treasure, I thanked the Lord when I saw the shiniest golden notebook I had ever seen, as if it had his name written all over it.

Soon enough it would, spelling out in raised letters the name of the man who had given me gifts beyond anything the world could offer, the one with a legacy yearning to be told.

Harry Mundine Walker.

I filled the pages with photos I had taken or collected over the years, including old snapshots pinned on the walls or hiding in drawers at the family home in Jubullum. From the 1950s to the present day, they lit up a life you wouldn't believe, unless you could see the places and faces they featured. In between lay Pop's favorite hymns and scripture, the ones he asked for in the *Intensive Care Unit*, as well as in the days and weeks that followed.

After months of cutting and pasting, and many long hours of pen to page, it was ready. Father's Day had just passed, as good a time as any to present what had begun to feel like a prized item. Out of the blue, I had a vision of gifting it to him at *his* Pop's grave, but I wasn't sure about asking and let the idea go as we landed in Jubullum, having lunch with him and the old girl, the family popping in and out to grab a feed. Then, with my travel buddy having a *yarn* with Ma on the porch, and the *jarjums* scattering for an afternoon outside, the moment had arrived.

"Remember when you were in hospital and I started that notebook?" I said, sitting by his side at the table.

"Yeah, yeah," he replied, with a curious look.

"Happy Father's Day," I said, placing the gift in his hands, wrapped up nice in a colorful cloth. He held it tight, turning to me with a face fixed on gratitude, but mixed with a touch of something else.

"This means so much to me," he said. "I wasn't sure if I would get anything for Father's Day, so I went to the store last weekend and bought *myself* a gift."

Overlooking the Road to the Old Racecourse in Tabulam

Seeing God redeem even the little things was a sight to behold, especially when it brought a smile to the old fella's face. But before I could allow the thought to settle, he continued, his eyes speaking wonders.

"All I wanted to do was go and visit my Pop's grave," he added. "But no one could take me."

Chills came over me as I returned his gaze.

"Pop, I was gonna ask if we go today," I said, almost in shock. "But I wasn't sure if it was right to ask."

His face lit up as he sat taller in his seat, looking at the clock hanging over the kitchen table, before replying with a vigor I hadn't seen all day.

"Do you still want to go?"

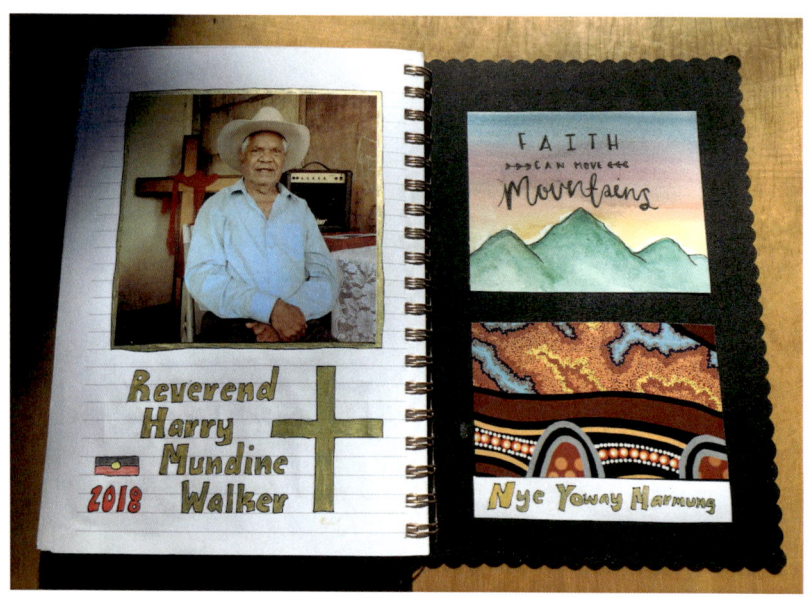

Excerpt from Pop's Golden Notebook

He grabbed his favorite cowboy hat, Gene Autry style, and I took the notebook under my arm as we jumped in the car for the short drive over the old wooden bridge and through town. The dirt road followed the ridge overlooking the river, and as we neared the Tabulam Racecourse, Pop pointed out the cemetery among a scattering of eucalyptus trees. We parked up and I followed him into the enclosed field where a few dozen grave sites lay in rough rows, up and down the grassy hill.

"This is it," Pop said, as we reached his old fella's resting place, standing quietly for a moment, before I handed him the gift once again, this time just as I had envisioned. He began to pray in Wahlubal, and I closed my eyes to listen, most of his words unknown to my ears, but the meaning as loud and clear as the empty fields around us were silent.

Suddenly I felt his hand touch my arm, softly and tenderly, as if referencing me in his prayer. He would tell me afterwards that he was introducing me to *his* Pop, sharing the story of what had taken place, from lying there in surgery to standing here today, saying *this is what he's done for me.*

Arriving home, we gathered on the porch as Pop unwrapped the glowing golden notebook with great expectation, touched to see his name in raised letters on the cover. He turned the pages and leafed through a history of his and Ma's life and spiritual journey, letting me know he was very proud of it. His great-grandson *Izaiah* hovered nearby, curious to see the insides of this new family heirloom.

"One day it could be yours," I said to the little fella, praying a generational bridge might be built by its gifting. Pop agreed with the sentiment as I showed him the blank pages where he could write out his favorite prayers in English, as well as translating them into Wahlubal, that the young ones might learn and share in times to come.

"You can read from it at *my* funeral," he said with a look of contentment, the book before him making clear he would be *leaving a legacy of gold.* It had been a year of dreaming and months in the making, but from that very first day in the hospital, to this last minute trip to the cemetery, it all seemed beyond anything we could have planned, a series of appointments in the Lord's timing, made possible by the timeless grace he extends to us, children of an Everlasting Father who needs nothing in return, but the gift of a willing heart, ready to receive.

The Reverend Harry Walker, 1992

TO BECOME THE REVEREND

So when they had appointed elders in every church, and prayed with fasting, they commended them to the Lord in whom they had believed.

Acts 14:23 NKJV

It was no ordinary ordination.

"Take a look at this," Pop said, folder in hand, pulling out an old news article.

It was an unlikely setting for a church ordination, the Tabulam Aboriginal settlement, but one befitting the historic occasion for the first Aboriginal person to be ordained in the Uniting Church in New South Wales.

I had heard of the milestone here and there, but having never seen documentation of the day itself, I could only guess at the details. Now, holding the article in my hands, seeing the eyes of a youthful Uncle Harry staring back at me, the importance of the occasion began to sink in.

...the people came in their droves, many driving for hours for the historic occasion when Pastor Harry Walker, the silver haired father of eight, and grandfather of 12, was to become The Reverend.

Pop and Ma had lived through revival in the 1950s and 60s, led by the elders who sowed into them the songs and scripture they would carry for a lifetime. After Pop was called to enter the ministry, and blessed to attend Bible College in Brisbane, he and Ma planted their *Boogilma*, good job, ministry over the range in South Lismore in 1978. It was now 1992 and Pop's leadership was being recognized in front of 400 guests, black and white, gathered for the first event ever held in the soon-to-be-opened sports center on the mission in Jubullum.

In 1788, the continent had been covered by hundreds of independent tribes and nations, a mighty civilization existing over great spans of time. But by the 21st century, their numbers had dwindled to 3% of the modern population. A great majority of those who remained, particularly the ones who managed to keep their culture thriving, lived in the remote areas of the North and West. The Eastern coastline, dotted with the state capitals of Brisbane, Sydney and Melbourne, along with the ever expanding sprawl of Western society, had come close to wiping the local indigenous population off the map in many places. Having grown up in mainstream Australia myself, it was extremely rare to see groups of black and white folks together, and my childhood was a case in point, with one notable exception.

My best friend, Bradley, was Aboriginal.

It was only now, being welcomed into the world of Pop and Ma, that I started to think of how my best friend's experience must have been so different from mine. I imagined the prejudice he must have faced,

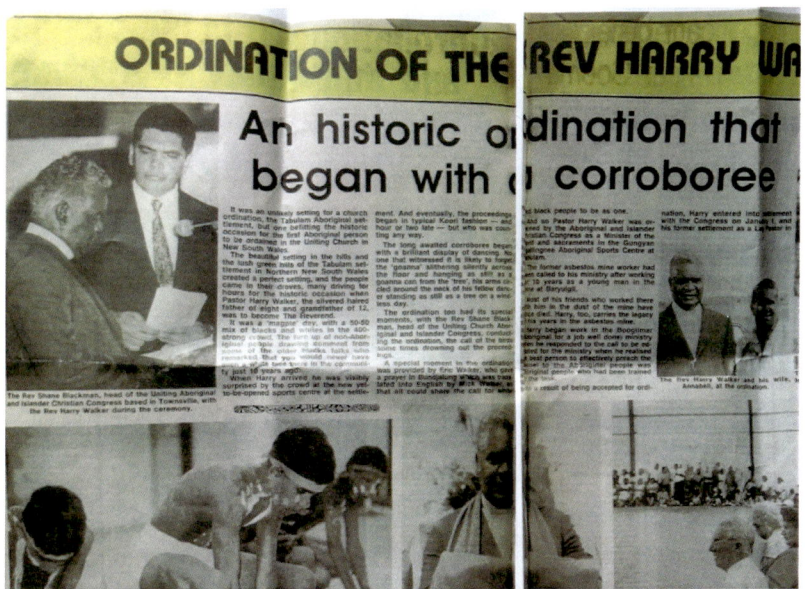
Koori Mail Article, 1992

the trials forced upon him, the complications of living between worlds that struggled to co-exist. Perhaps the reason I felt so comfortable with Pop was how much he reminded me of Bradley, someone from a different culture, a different kind of family, yet someone who I had loved, and now missed dearly, having lost touch with the boy who felt like the brother I never had.

After growing up in the ways of the Wahlubal, immersed in traditional language and culture, many of Pop's first interactions with the *whitefella* had been the farmers in and around Tabulam, the ones who had settled in his ancestral home, bringing foreign animals and colonial customs at war with their way of life. Despite some of the horrors inflicted upon their people, he would take steps to note the kind things they did, speaking fondly of the ones who

Harry Walker's Achievement, Unknown Publication

offered him and his uncles work in the local fields and forests, chopping wood or ringbarking. Hearing him speak this way, the modern Chief of an ancient tribe, a leader tasked with steering through storms of change, Pop seemed determined to embody the spirit of reconciliation. His calling into the church, and the tireless ministry he would undertake with his dear Annabelle, would endear him to a generation of white preachers, pastors and congregants up and down the Eastern coastline. Some of them would become lifelong friends, brothers and sisters in the Lord, having erased a cultural divide achingly prevalent in society.

I had heard that *all things shall be reconciled in Christ*, thinking it a spiritual teaching for ages to come, but seeing it now clearly alive in the bonds Pop and Ma had forged with the faithful, *called out ones of many colors*. As I read about the day Pop had been made

Reverend, it seemed more than a public recognition of a title, or the celebration of a man called into higher leadership for his people. This felt like reconciliation in action, a ray of hope for cross-cultural healing, a bridge to a future where color and race might separate no more.

It was a 'magpie' day, with a 50-50 mix of blacks and whites in the 400-strong crowd. The turn up of non-Aboriginal people drawing comment from some of the older black folks who remarked that you would never have seen a white face there in the community just 10 years ago.

This truly was historic, an event that Pop and the community would treasure for years to come. His memory of it would still be alive 25 years later, when another crowd of many colors would come in droves to that same sports center, gathering to welcome an international delegation arriving to honor the man now known as *The Chief*, as well as *The Reverend*. This time I would be their host, but Pop would most certainly be the hero of the day once again.

News excerpts are from the Koori Mail, Wednesday March 11, 1992

A magpie is a common Australian bird with black and white features

Pop with Chief Phil Lane Jr, Jubullum, 2018

THEY STOOD CHIEF TO CHIEF

Return to me, for I have redeemed you.

Isaiah 44:22

The Chief stepped out of the van.

His Native American headdress standing tall, fan of many feathers in hand, he strode with purpose across the field to meet the man he had come to see.

Poppy Harry Walker.

They stood Chief to Chief, beaming as if lifelong friends, onlookers in awe of the scene. One by one, I introduced the delegation to Pop, visitors from across the globe sharing hugs and shaking hands with the Chief of this land.

We entered the old sports center to see hundreds of friends and family gathered from across the region, and I was promptly handed a microphone. I told the crowd why we had come, the great journeys our guests had taken, and how grateful we were to be there honoring their elders, and their country.

Then I handed the mic to Pop.

"I've waited 70 years for this," he said. "Because when we were little boys playing up and down the river here, you know what our favorite game was?"

"Cowboys and Indians!" he shouted, the crowd howling in laughter. "And after all these years I finally got to meet the *real* Chief."

Our guests from afar shared a speech or a song, and then it came time to wrap up the official program, a feast about ready to be served at the far end of the hall. Thinking on the spot of a good way to close, I invited everyone to stand and join us in singing Pop and Ma's favorite old hymn.

Ngai Yoway! Yoway! Yoway!
Ngai Yoway Marmung

I say Yes! Yes! Yes!
I say Yes, Lord

A sea of voices filled the space, and it felt as if the walls had joined in the choir, echoing as they must have done at Pop's ordination a quarter century ago. Days like this had grown rare in recent times, and seeing the smiles on so many faces, knowing there would be stories to tell for months or years to come, it felt like a few rays of hope came in on the back of the sun shining through the rafters.

As groups gathered for selfies with the Native American Chief, I noticed a bunch of young Aboriginal men I'd never met, imagining they must have come in from other communities. But when Uncle Kev came over to thank me for putting on the

The Sports Center at Jubullum, 2018

event, what he said made the whole thing complete in a way we couldn't have planned when the visit first came into view. The young men were from *Balund-a*, the culturally based diversionary program for incarcerated Aboriginal youth just down the river. I looked again and thought of what this day must have meant for them, not only free to be with their families, but to see their community and their Chief honored in such a way. Their eyes seemed to shine a little brighter as we bid them farewell, windows into the Almighty's redemptive heart, restoring lives and villages, one broken piece put back together at a time.

Two days later, Pop would shake the hand of the visiting Chief once again, cameras flashing as he crossed the stage to greet his new friend from afar, this time in front of a thousand people gathered for the big *Unity Earth* festival on the coast.

Pop and Ma at the Unity Earth Festival, 2018

"I am Poppy Harry Walker," he faced the crowd, packed under a big red tent that kept the blazing sun at bay. "I guess many of you know who I am."

Recounting our visit to Jubullum that week, he spoke of the blessing it was to have such an esteemed international delegation visit *their* community way out in the bush, going off the beaten track to pay respect to the country he called home. Most of all, nailing his *Cowboys and Indians* laugh line a second time, he shared how grateful he was to fulfill that childhood dream of meeting a Native American Chief, even more so that this one had come to *his* land, to meet *him*.

Pop may have joked about waiting 70 years for it, but there seemed another side to that coin, as if some had waited a lifetime to meet *him*, this legendary character holding the torch for his people of old. He had held his head high through ups and downs, the legacy of his language and the faith of his elders showing him where to look for the strength he would need to see through the storms of life on the mission. Soon a new generation of Wahlubal would arise, young men like those we had met at the hall this week, young women with the fire to carry the torch into the future. That was for their hands to receive, to steward, and to pass on as their ancestors have done for thousands of years.

But in Pop's other hand was the torch of *The Way*, the one he and Ma had tended for half a century, the fire with the force to free weary souls, near and far. If my time with them had taught me anything, it was to say *Yes* when called to serve, even if it meant making sacrifices that were hard to explain, or being sent on a journey into the unknown. For six years this torch had lit my path, enough for me to trust in another six and beyond, wherever the twists might take the story, and whatever the cost to bring it home.

From those first teachings in the hospital, through the depths of discipleship, in the moments and messages written on the tablet of my heart, and the legacy captured in a pair of golden notebooks, from reading about the day Pop became *The Reverend*, to bringing new friends from across the globe, the torch that had fueled it all was the one he and Ma were placing in my hands, and I could do no more in life than to take it without question, to pass it on freely, and to pray the Almighty might shine upon all those who say *Yes* to feeling the warmth of its flame.

You know the way to the place where I am going.

JOHN 14:4

THE JOURNEY
Part Three

Memorial of Moses, Mount Nebo, Jordan

EXODUS OF THE HEART

He will lead us into that land,
a land flowing with milk and honey.

Numbers 14:8

Moses had stood on this mountain.

I looked out from Mount Nebo in modern day Jordan, the land of Ancient Canaan far off in the distance, wondering what the aging prophet must have felt all those centuries ago as he caught a glimpse of the Promised Land for the first time.

After leading his people out of Egypt, they had wandered the wilderness for 40 years, trusting the hand of the Almighty upon their lives, but aching for the journey to be over. How they must have longed for that land of milk and honey, the place their future generations would come to know as Israel.

Seeing the hills roll into the horizon, I thought of the view coming over the range into Jubullum, and how it had always looked like a Promised Land to me. I even recalled the sensation of escaping the captivity of modern life, heart set on a place far from the city lights and luxuries we take for granted, only to find out they were the things keeping us captive.

Back in the day, Pop and Ma's ancestors would walk from horizon to horizon, traveling to and from great gatherings of tribes and nations, leaving a trail of fruit forests and stories for the ages, handed down from old to young, much as the Israelites had done in a land far across the sea. To the Wahlubal, all land was sacred, a representation of, and belonging to, the Maker and Sustainer of all. It was He who had made *this* land of milk and honey, and they had been raised from the dust of the earth to care for it.

But things had changed since the foreigners arrived, their freedom to hunt and cultivate their surrounds, to live and to thrive as they had for thousands of years, gone within a handful of lifetimes. The ancient home of the Wahlubal, like so many others across the continent, had come under new management, and their way of life, along with the culture that fueled it, was being forced into captivity. Pop had been the last boy born while the tribe still lived by the river, before they were moved onto the mission, much like the reservation of America. As a youngster, his old people could remember what it was like to live in freedom, stewards of a Garden of Eden that gave them everything they ever needed, the mountains and valleys crafted by a Creator their peoples had known since the beginning.

So, much like the ancient Israelites, slaves to the Pharaohs of Egypt, or later, held firm under the yoke of Roman rule, there must have been a longing for the Wahlubal to overthrow the system that had come to oppress them, and to live in freedom once more. For centuries, the Hebrew people had prayed for a savior, their long prophesied *messiah*, to rise up as a

The Sacred Land known today as Australia

great military and political leader, destined to drive out the oppressors and restore the land and people to glory. So when a country Rabbi named Yeshua, better known as Jesus the Nazarene, came to fulfill this prayer, claim His Lordship, and administer this Kingdom of God that was at hand, many of his generation were gravely disappointed to learn that his would be a revolution of the spirit.

Not only would this King *not* overthrow Roman rule, he would lead his followers out of captivity through a gate so narrow, they would have to leave behind almost everything they thought was valuable, taking a leap of faith into a realm where surrender and sacrifice were more powerful than spears and arrows. Unlike the physical escape from Egypt, this would be an *exodus of the heart*, freedom *from* the ways of this world, an invitation to *eternal* life.

Room of the Last Supper, Jerusalem, 2020

Rather than raising swords against their enemy, Jesus had called his disciples to pray for them, to turn the other cheek, to willingly walk the extra mile. This King's battle plan favored forgiveness over uprising, a humble heart willing to confess that God alone can restore our true sovereignty, putting us on the path to a freedom unconquerable by any person, nation or empire.

Pop himself had become Chief to a great people on the blunt end of colonization, with stories of displacement still richly embedded in the minds of those who were asked to remember. But his was a story of redemption as well as loss, each chapter a river of memories that would all, in turn and in time, arrive at the one great ocean to which his old people had pointed the way. Despite the hardships of life on the mission, the lives and ways of life lost, they had gathered, sometimes three times a day, to sing, to pray, and to praise the One who had come to meet them in *their* Promised Land, the Peacemaker with the power to calm any storm and loosen any shackle, not for a day or a season, but in ways everlasting.

The *whitefella* called him Jesus, they called him *Balagahn*, the handsome one. He was the fulfillment of the Law of Moses, the Son of Man lifted up on a tree in Jerusalem, his name now lifted up in praise halfway around the globe by an ancient peoples who, like the Israelites, had come to know captivity, and who, like billions of others, had come to know a freedom in Him that could never be taken away. At first, the disciples of Jesus would fret at the talk of his leaving, but hearing they could partake of His goodness through the feast served at the last supper, they would be comforted knowing no hunger could ever compete with a heart that knows how to feast upon the bread of life.

One day far off in the future would come another disciple, the last boy born before his people were moved onto the mission, the husband and father who overcame the odds to emerge as Reverend and Chief, a man lifted up on the mountainous shoulders of his old people to catch a glimpse, not of a Promised Land far off on the horizon, but of a God who had never left or forsaken them, a Savior who had suffered to show them *The Way*, and a King who had come to set His people free.

Church of the Holy Sepulchre, 2020

TOMB OF THE RISEN ONE

Praise the Lord, O Jerusalem!

Psalm 147:12

The Old City was deserted.

Winding through the streets of Jerusalem, it seemed like history had been written on every corner, the ancient stones beneath my feet worn down in places by countless steps taken on pilgrimage.

The maze of alleys and archways narrowed to an opening so tiny it almost concealed the grandeur on the other side, the aged sign hanging over the entrance the only hint at the destination awaiting.

The Church of the Holy Sepulchre.

Stepping through the doors that had opened and closed for century after century, I made my way to the high domed atrium housing the tomb of Jesus. I had visited many times in the months prior, weaving through walls of tourists to catch a glimpse of a relic, or the briefest time to reflect, before being waved on by another sea of phone cameras.

But this time, I was the lone pilgrim.

A *Unity Earth* event had brought me to the Holy Land, but I had felt the call to stay, a few extra days turning into weeks, then months. That was the year they shut half the world down, and by now the bustling streets of Jerusalem were eerily quiet, shop after shop in the famous Old City market abandoned by their owners and operators, for lack of clientele.

The handful who remained rushed out to urge me into their establishment, those tourists that fueled the trade among the sea of tiny streets had all but vanished, and they were struggling to feed their families. I wasn't here to shop, but I bought what I could, knowing a sale of any size would help.

A young family had rented me an apartment in what felt like a thousand year old building, with hobbit sized doors and a courtyard shared by a half dozen others. During my work breaks, I would walk around the corner to pray in the *Holy Sepulchre*, often kneeling on the cold stone floor, taking in the palatial surrounds of the spot considered the site of the cross, the historical *Golgotha*. Other times I would sit quietly on the wooden benches in the back of the Ethiopian annex, at home in the rustic surroundings, leaning into the scent of incense and the glow of candles lit for loved ones far away.

I kept Pop and Ma close in my prayers, stretching to imagine them visiting this place, one they had heard of a thousand times, but would never see, or be seen in. That said, I pulled up a photo of the three of us and placed it in front of the tomb of their beloved Savior, snapping a photo of their likeness at the peak of pilgrimage sites for a follower of *The Way*.

The Old City of Jerusalem seen from the Mount of Olives, 2020

You could hear a pin drop in the silence enveloping the mighty stone walls of the complex originally consecrated in 335 AD, light rays pouring through the dome above the sanctuary, adding to a sense of otherworldliness. The magnitude of quiet took me back to those precious times with Pop, waiting on him to put words to the experience of knowing God in the spaces between, glimmers from beyond that reveal to us who He is, and who we are in Him.

I exited onto the great stone courtyard, glimmering in the midday sun, still surprised to see it without the sign waving tour guides and their backpacked groups speaking a hundred and one languages. Climbing the steps at the far end, I searched for a bar or two of phone reception, dialing the number for the house in Jubullum, and hearing the old fella's voice on the other end of the line.

Pop and Ma at the Tomb of the Holy One, 2020

"Wahlubal," he answered.

"Pop, it's Adam, guess where I'm calling from?" I paused, giving him a moment to consider the options. "*The Church of the Holy Sepulchre!*".

"Gee, hey!" he replied, laughing.

"From Jerusalem to Jubullum," I added. "Who would have thought?"

The flame of the faithful had swept through his village in the 1950s, fueling Pop and Ma's journey ever since, until the day they would call me out of the world to carry the torch as they had for so long. They were the ones who had invested in me a reverence for the teachings and trials of the One who's life and death had made this place the focal point of prayer and pilgrimage for millions. To be here, at *the tomb of the Risen One*, was a brush with history so close you could kneel and kiss the stone where the Master's body had lain, tourists arising with tears in their eyes, fulfilling the desire to walk in the steps of the Savior who suffered on this soil.

Pop and Ma's candle of faith had made it back to the place where darkness was overcome once and for all, where the light of the world was thought to be quenched and found to be unquenchable, rising to shine so bright that eyes of any color could see the truth behind the veil He had torn. They may not have made it in person, but I prayed they would find comfort in knowing their godson had held them close when his feet touched the ground at Calvary.

Within days, my Holy Land stay drawing to a close, I walked the streets of the Old City one final time, so quiet I could hear my footsteps on the paths of stone, my spirit heavy at the thought of leaving. But as I saw the events that had positioned me to be here in such a way, at such a time, I prayed that whatever my heart had heard in the silence of Jerusalem, was a gift I could now carry to the ends of the earth.

Most importantly, I would bring it all the way home to Jubullum, to our dear Pop and Ma, followers of the faith that had emerged from these same winding streets in the 1st century AD, where Jesus had walked and talked and given his life that ours might have hope eternal, for from the tomb he rose, the King who calms the storms, the One who speaks in the stillness, the Man who wraps His loving arms around us pilgrims on *The Way*.

At Masada, Overlooking the Dead Sea, 2020

THIS FORTRESS OF FAITH

For You are my rock and my fortress.

Psalm 31:3

This was a perch that touched the sky.

A mountain rising from the desert, cliffs on all sides, no force could possibly scale and conquer this high ground. You would need a mountain sized ramp just to try, a prospect beyond hope, unless you had the wealth and willingness of an empire behind you.

And so it was in 70 AD, after the overthrow of Jerusalem and scattering of the Jewish communities throughout the known world, that a legendary final stand would take place.

960 men, women and children had holed up on the hilltop complex known as *Masada*, holding off the might of the Imperial Army for three years. The only solution for the 8000-strong legion led by *Flavius Silva*, was to conquer the cliffs and meet these courageous holdouts on level ground, knowing their resistance would finally be futile.

And so a ramp it was, but lacking the time and technology to construct from iron, brick or stone, they started with old fashioned soil and rock, digging and stacking, digging and stacking, until their helmets could see over the fortifications.

We sat on the ancient stone steps of a meeting place that once was, high on top of the mountain, tourists snapping photos and gazing over the Dead Sea to the East. I imagined what it must have been like for those warriors and their families, holed up in the clouds, knowing their final battle was upon them.

40 years earlier, Yeshua had prophesied the fall of the temple, and the scattering of the tribes of Israel, his crucifixion failing to kill the words and *The Way* he planted in the hearts of those who would follow in His steps. For here we were, 2,000 years in the future, calling on the name of the One who had been rejected by the authorities of His time, but upon whose shoulder the government would rest forever.

For even the army of an empire was no match for the legions of angels dispatched to protect the hearts of the faithful in times of despair, or the love of the Almighty who would part seas and deliver lands of milk and honey into the hands of those who walk in the way of righteousness. He was the defender of the weak and weary, the healer of pain and breaker of chains who would fight to free every last one of us.

Pop and Ma, and the elders of Jubullum, like so many leaders of Aboriginal tribes across the continent, had seen the march of progress approaching, the armies of industry plucking treasures from the land they knew as sacred. And though the new seats of power had been set in the

The Ramp Built the Roman Army at Masada, 2020

cities on the coast, their living temple of Creation falling field by field around them, far over the ranges and across the plains, there were the last ones standing, Original Peoples holding onto their ways of old. As the realities grew dire, they would circle up around fires, lock arms with their brethren, and stand firm on the mountain of their mission to preserve and protect their tribes and traditions, their language and laughter, the lands and the water that had nourished them since the beginning.

And though it seemed a given that one day these forces of the future would ascend the cliffs of their resistance, seeking the subtle or outright dismantling of the remnants they held onto, for Pop and Ma, and the elders of *The Way*, there remained a freedom that could never be taken, for He who dwelled in them had already overcome the world.

Amongst the Ruins of Masada, 2020

That hope would fuel their fight, bringing courage in crisis, defending the heart from fear. As a handful of the scattered had once made *Masada* a fortress in the sky, so too had these elders scaled the Rock of Ages, *this fortress of faith* from where we can hold off the enemy that seeks to scale the cliffs of the human heart, that darkness on a quest to quench the light of the world, only to be reminded that it lost that battle at the cross, and the war for the weary is fought in the heavens, where no army, human or otherwise, could ever top our Lord God Almighty.

But our human condition is fragile, and with the Roman legion on the verge of victory, all but two women and five children at *Masada* would take their own lives, for to be lost to sword or slavery would surely break their spirits. April 15, 73 AD would go down as a win for the empire, squashing the remains of a rebellion that had begun seven years prior, and all but ended with the fall of Jerusalem in 70 AD. The courageous plight of those who extended the battle through another three turnings of the seasons, would go down as a historic last stand. But for those souls lost to the hand of their own, whatever the portion of pride knowing their stand had stood beyond the realm of possibility, it must have been mixed with the burden of a battle they knew they could not win, and the fear of an unknown journey awaiting.

Pop and Ma had found peace in the moving of God's spirit through their community, no matter the chaos or crisis of an encroaching civilization that was quickly overtaking their own. Like the rebels of *Masada*, they could see the danger incoming, but their perch on high was the Lord's eagle eye view, the perspective of heaven with which they could see the unseen at work in any battle, and to sing with confidence, knowing their destiny was in His arms.

Rock of ages, cleft for me, let me hide myself in thee

As the sun set, we descended the mountain in silence, dust and desert as far as the eyes could see. But hearing the stories of what had taken place atop these cliffs, one could look within to see all the sights you would ever need. Admiration for the strength of the scattered, love for those lost in the end, and a determination to share the saving power of a *messiah* who may not have saved the temple in Jerusalem, or halted the legion in its tracks, but had built us a ramp to God's heavenly mountain, from where we get our strength, and to where we go to find sanctuary everlasting.

Queen Liliʻuokalani

MEET US AT THE PALACE

*In their hearts humans plan their course,
but the Lord establishes their steps.*

Proverbs 16:9

The stars would lead them here.

Ancient Polynesian explorers, stewards of the mightiest of oceans, coming to land, live and plant abundantly in the volcanic soil of the islands to be known as Hawai'i.

Their descendants would build a kingdom, united by Kamehameha the Great in 1810, and welcomed into the family of nations in the decades to follow. Visitors would come from afar, seeking supplies for their arduous trade journeys, or sandalwood for the markets in *Canton*. Some would stay, bringing intrigue and industry, others would land with the gospel at heart, and revival at hand.

My task had been much simpler as I scanned the islands for sunshine, seeking a few days of refuge before flying on to America. I booked a room on the North Shore of *O'ahu* for three nights, and set off with a suitcase and a backpack, landing at Honolulu International Airport at 6am on a Sunday.

That was five years ago.

I looked up at the mountains, still coming to terms with how the island had drawn me in that very first morning. The last second diversion to *Waikiki* on the way out of the airport, the choice to shun the GPS and drive halfway across the island in the wrong direction. The gridlock traffic from an accident on the two-lane country road, forcing me to backtrack into *Wahiawa*, searching for a restroom. The first café that appeared on the map, the decision to order some tea and a snack, to notice the book shelf, the titles and names, and to know in a flash that my morning of misadventure now had a shot at becoming the adventure of a lifetime.

All the books were about God.

The tide of my day turned right side up, and I asked one of the staff if she could tell me about the place I had landed. She pointed to a table nearby, saying I should talk to the old fella Tom who, with his wife Cindy, had launched the *Surfing The Nations* ministry, and its flagship *Surfers Coffee,* a pit stop miraculously planted on my path. Pulling up a photo of Pop and Ma, I told him about our journey unfolding, and he suggested I look into a Hawaiian church program that took place once a year, calling over someone who might know more. We looked it up and the planets fell into place as I read about the event and its organizers, their story resonating so vividly with our own. But when I saw the dates for the program that year, I had no option, but to do a double take.

It was starting today and going all week.

On the Island of O'ahu, 2019

I gasped, a mix of awe with a dose of disbelief, texting the number on the website to ask about the possibility of participating. "Yes," came the reply from Aunty Brenda, not more than a few minutes later. "*Meet us at the palace* on Friday."

This would be my first lived experience of *aloha*, of being welcomed by a string of strangers in a place I had barely set foot on. Years later I would return with a story to tell the old fella whose café had pointed to a plan beyond our own making, a step we couldn't have established, unless it had been placed by the hand of the One who puts us where He wants us to be. There would be ups and downs, and oceans to cross and cross again, but this island was to become much more than a stopover.

Our visit to the palace would convince me of that.

'Iolani Palace in Honolulu

This had been home to the Hawaiian monarchy before the overthrow in 1893, the site from where they stewarded their people, their culture, and their kingdom, at least so it was, until foreign business interests intervened. I thought of Pop and how the Wahlubal Chiefs before him had been dispossessed of their ancestral lands by strangers from afar, and though separated by half an ocean, the descendants of both peoples were still riding out the ripple effects of colonization.

I approached a group gathered near the gift shop, a little nervously, asking if I was in the right place. One by one, they greeted me with warmth, making me feel at home in their family of grace and *aloha*. We entered the stately building, hitting play on audio descriptions of each regal room, historical artifact, and 19th century wardrobe piece, before gathering upstairs for the finale to our visit. It was then that one of the group leaders handed me a songbook, and told me to open to *The Queen's Prayer*.

Liliʻuokalani had been stripped of her power by a "provisional government" initiated by sugar barons, and backed by U.S. force. After a group of royalists made moves to reclaim the kingdom, she had been imprisoned in a room here at *ʻIolani Palace*, the one we were about to enter. This was a black mark in history, a reminder that imperialism had won the day again, the consequences still played out by the great great grandchildren of her generation.

So when the Queen took out her pen on March 22, 1895, the loss, the anger, and the resentment was still fresh in the air over Honolulu. But as I followed our group into the aptly named *Imprisonment Room*, I sensed there was more to this story, and more to this song. We formed a circle around the perimeter and I fell into place as my new friends lifted their voices.

ʻO kou aloha no
A ia i ka lani

Oh! Lord thy loving mercy
Is high as the heavens

It was breathtaking, unlike anything I had ever heard, and not at all what I would have expected from a song written at a time of such injustice, by a leader taken captive in her own home. My eyes closed, I began to hear weeping, as if the Queen's own descendants had returned to sit by her feet, grieving together the loss of their nation.

Ko'u noho mihi ana
A pa'ahao ia

Whilst humbly meditating
Within these walls imprisoned

Lili'uokalani had not wavered from the faith she embraced as a young princess-to-be decades earlier, knowing that the grace and mercy of God were needed now more than ever. And with that faith at hand, she had penned a song that would uplift the hearts of her people and their offspring for generations to come.

Aka e huikala
A ma'ema'e no

Forgive with loving kindness
That we might be made pure

Hearing it felt more like a beginning than a painful end, a pivot to a world of hope where the hearts of the people could never be imprisoned, if only we might seek out and enter the narrow gate, where forgiveness brings peace, no matter the situation.

Ko makou maluhia
A mau loa aku

And peace will be our portion
Now and forever more

I had entered this room unsure of what lay ahead, but I left it knowing my life would never be the same, and that maybe, just maybe, I was being

The Queen's Prayer, originally Ke Aloha o Ke Haku (The Lord's Mercy)

prompted to live some of it out here, in this place, with this family. There would be more journeys to take, and the guiding lights of Pop and Ma to support with all my might, but these first few days in Hawai'i had made me wonder whether the Lord had brought me here to bring me home, for a season or two, or perhaps forever more.

Either way, from that moment, hearing our new friends sing *The Queen's Prayer*, what started with three nights would become five years and counting, our visit to the palace emerging as a pillar in a story unfolding across the globe, from the village of Jubullum to the old city of Jerusalem, and now to Honolulu, the island city from where the Kings and Queens of Hawai'i once reigned.

Aunty Blanche's Homeless Village in Waimānalo

ISLANDS OF LIVING HOPE

*The righteous will inherit
the land and dwell in it forever.*

Psalm 37:29

They were a heavenly audience.

Called up to sing at a homeless village fair on the East Side of O‘ahu, I snuck in a few of Pop and Ma's old favorites, hoping they would go over OK.

I come to the garden alone

A group of Aunties joined in with joy on the chorus, one of them grabbing her ukulele to strum along.

And…he…walks with me, and he talks with me

Chatting with a stall holder after my set, I was invited back for church on Sunday, arriving to a sight straight out of Jubullum, young and old gathered at picnic tables under a tent in the field.

Their *Kahu* greeted me warmly, asking me to stand and introduce myself, and I shared all about Pop and Ma, the Aboriginal revival of the 1950s and 60s, and the torch they were leaving for us to carry on.

A fleet of ukuleles took flight as the Aunties led worship, singing *Leaning On The Everlasting Arms*, just as they did back home. This was *Kūpuna Church*, meaning elders church in Hawaiian, and my heart was filled to know the Lord had made a way for me to be with these new friends, in my new home.

Breaking bread after a service filled with good learning and lots of laughter, I would offer my support for Aunty Blanche, a mighty woman of God who had brought the houseless home to live in this village of hope and prayer. Within minutes I was recruited to join the PR committee for the next fair, and I would return for a meeting that week, joining a circle of servants with a shared heart to love on the residents there. When someone asked what I would be doing to help, the Aunty who had recruited me surprised us with her answer, skipping the technical details to get to the heart of the matter.

"You know, I think God has sent him," she said, leaning back in her chair, hinting that was all we needed to know, and taking me back to my first *cuppa* with Ma, all those years ago, as if the story was closing its own loop. From Jubullum to Hawai'i, I had followed the call to serve the elders, but as always, they knew much better than I did, that it was the Lord putting me to work in the way He wanted.

Soon that would include *River of Life Mission*, who after 35 years and 12 million meals served, were now working with local churches to start homeless ministry hubs all over the island. Visiting the mission for the first time, I shared how one of the first songs I'd learned from Ma was *River of Life*, and

Singing River of Life for 100 Church Leaders, 2023

they took me straight down to their weekly chapel service to share it with the staff. Weeks later I would sing it again, for 100 pastors, partners and volunteers gathered for an island-wide leaders dinner. And in the year to come, I would immerse myself in the ministry, coordinating the development of the new *Road to Redemption* initiative, a movement to mobilize a generation of the faithful, equipping them to serve the suffering on the streets.

The horrific wildfires on Maui in August of 2023 would shock the islands, and we did what we could to respond, supporting locally run relief programs, including a project to build tiny homes for survivors. The first recipient was a young mother-to-be, expecting any day now, and no longer having to come home from the hospital to a tent outside a house she was sharing with 18 others.

Pacific Islands Forum in Rarotonga, 2023

It was a small thing in the scope of the disaster, and I had played a small role in it, but seeing the subtle move of God through the ministries in which we were serving, gave me hope that even a little bit could change a life for the better.

The more we pulled on the thread of these and other challenges, most all seemed to stem from January of 1893, when the people had lost the oversight of their land and future. Learning how central the issue was to every other, I would be put into service for Uncle Leon, an elder statesman of the movement to restore the kingdom. Hearing him speak so vividly of the pre-annexed islands as a sovereign, flourishing, *Christian* nation, one had to wonder if their mission for independence was just as inevitable as it might sound impossible at first hearing.

That said, the worldly odds stacked against them made clear that victory would flow only from the mighty hand of God, the One they had turned to for guidance in the establishment of their nation. The Constitution of 1840, Hawai'i's first, would require no laws be passed that were at odds with God's law, its Declaration of Rights opening with a message steeped in biblical wisdom.

"God hath made of one blood all nations of men to dwell on the earth," in unity and blessedness.

Soon the quest would take me to *Rarotonga*, where the Cook Islands was playing host to the *Pacific Islands Forum*. In meeting with dignitaries and local leaders, the talk around self-determination for the peoples of Oceania seemed widespread, and growing in momentum. But as much as the levers of power must be pulled, and the excesses of extractive policies rewritten, man or woman alone could never do what can be done by the Almighty, and when trusting in Him, as so many around the Pacific are known to do, there will always be hope to anchor the soul of those striving for freedom.

As vast and complex as the challenges were, these places the Lord had called us to serve were like *islands of living hope,* and though many of them seemed to push on the bounds of possibility, the thing they had in common was the secret to their success, for those in the trenches knew to *Lean on the Everlasting Arms* of the One they had placed at the helm of their works, knowing He alone is the master of making the impossible come true.

My Te Āti Awa Great Grandmother

PEACE IN THE VALLEY

Blessed are the peacemakers.

Matthew 5:9

Our final destination awaited.

An ancient harbor on the North Island of New Zealand, the place where the *Tainui Waka* had landed many moons ago, their descendants destined to become Kings and Queens of the Māori.

Helmed by a master navigator named *Hoturoa*, that great voyaging vessel had followed the stars to a new life on the shores of *Aotearoa*, the land of the long white cloud. Through centuries of settlement, first their own, then that of the *pakeha* who brought much suffering and strife, the people of *Kawhia (kah-fee-ya)* remained courageous in their commitment to their children, their culture, and their *kaumātua*.

Their story, and the way they had overcome the crisis of colonization, was reminiscent of the trials Pop and Ma and so many Aboriginal communities had endured, the weight of change and uncertainty never fully breaking the backs of their spirit.

I had been invited to join a delegation from Hawai'i, visiting *maraes* across the North Island to study the traditional Māori community model. Launching out from the YWAM base in Auckland, we traveled through city and country, my left-side-of-the-road Aussie driving experience placing me at the wheel of a rickety old Econovan. As we prepared to rest before our final drive to *Kawhia* in the morning, I pulled out my ukulele and sang a Red Foley gospel hit from the 1940s, one I'd picked up while song hunting with Pop at the kitchen table in Jubullum.

There will be peace in the valley for me someday

It had become my hands down favorite, and I played it everywhere I went, from churches to concerts, birthdays to prayer nights, morning, evening and in between. The song seemed to work in any situation, whether the listener was hearing the words or not, coming across as a catchy country tune for some, speaking of life eternal to others.

"You have to sing that for my father when we get to *Kawhia*," I heard one of our hosts, a Māori uncle say. "He loves Red Foley."

Now I had heard a few hum along to the chorus, or register a nod of recollection, but other than Pop, I didn't know anyone who knew of Red Foley, let alone that I was doing his take on *Peace in the Valley*. These sure seemed like our kind of people, and I grew excited to meet them as we sat in a big circle on the *marae* in *Kawhia* the next day, listening intently to our host, a modern day *Hoturoa*, named after the one who had guided his people here so long ago. After a

With Aunty Bubby in Kawhia, 2023

while, he pulled out a vintage ukulele, singing a Hawaiian song before passing it on, and one by one those gathered would share whatever was on their heart. When it came my turn, a Māori Aunty across the room pointed at me with a smile.

"You're the Red Foley fella, aren't you?" she said, and as I launched into the song, she jumped out of her seat and danced over to me, where we swayed and sang out the words at the top of our lungs.

There'll be no sorrow, no sadness, no trouble I see

The circle erupted with cheers, and I learned later that the vibrant Aunty Bubby we instantly fell in love with, hadn't been singing so much of late. Our meeting had been a blessing to us both, and in the days that followed, I sat with her and her husband,

With Aunty Linda Ohia in Waikawa, 2023

the lovers of Red Foley and beyond, singing through the list of old hymns I had learned from Pop and Ma, while their family, friends and members of our delegation gathered around us in the dining hall. Days later, I would receive a video of them at home, Aunty Bubby still buzzing as she led them in a rousing *Peace in the Valley* on the guitar.

Til the Lord comes to call me away, oh yes

Hearing of her passing a year later, my eyes would tear as I imagined the immense loss for her family, as well as the community in and around *Kawhia*, grateful we were able to shine the tiniest of lights into each other's lives, in the short time we had together. Singing with Aunty and her husband had been the highlight of my trip, but as our delegation prepared to head home for Hawai'i, my journey was far from over, thanks to Aunty's daughter Karen, the one who had brought us to *Kawhia,* and who would now be taking me all the way to meet my own Māori tribe for the very first time. Our ancestors had sailed on the *Tokomaru,* settling within the snow capped sight of *Mount Taranaki,* before territorial battles and the sale of land had landed them in *Waikawa,* a village down the road from picturesque *Picton* on the North East tip of the South Island. But that was all I knew, having been raised in Australia without a present day connection to my great great great grandmother's tribe, the *Te Āti Awa.* Our Polynesian heritage had been passed down as a fun family fact, but not *one* had returned to our ancestral home since my great grandmother left for Queensland in 1909.

Joining the delegation had opened a door to change that, and I planned to stay a few extra days after the group left, making my way to *Waikawa* to take in some sights, perhaps even track down the tribal historian who might tell me more about our *whakapapa,* or genealogy. But as destiny would have it, though the town was a tiny dot on the South Island map, Karen said she had a friend there who was *Te Āti Awa* herself, someone who would be happy to reconnect me with the tribe, someone who, if I could have chosen one person out of the *five million* in Aotearoa to meet, it's quite possible I would have chosen her, the founding mother of the *World Christian Gathering on Indigenous Peoples.*

With her husband Monte Ohia, Aunty Linda had launched the historic event in the 1990s, inviting indigenous believers worldwide to gatherings in Aotearoa, South Dakota, Hawai'i and elsewhere. I had seen glimpses of faith and culture reconciled, from the Chief who took me to church, to hearing *The Queen's Prayer* sung at *'Iolani Palace* in Honolulu. But the impact of these gatherings was immense, and the stories I heard from Aunty as she hosted me in her home would seed a longing to experience something of that magnitude one day. I shared with her the story of meeting Pop and Ma, of being adopted as a son, of the torch being passed from their generation to ours, and the journey that had taken their tale halfway around the globe.

She reached over and handed me a thin book titled *One Lord, Different Cultures*, the Aboriginal art and photos on the cover instantly jumping out at me. This was a recap of their third gathering, held for the first time in Australia in the year 2000, and as I flipped through the pages my eyes lit up at the sight of First Nations faith warriors praising God while honoring and celebrating their native traditions. Reading the speeches captured in the book, I noticed one that sounded strangely familiar, scanning it again to try and make the connection.

I thank God I'm Aboriginal and proud to be one! God gave me back my pride and dignity. As I walk down the street with a lot of white people, I walk with my head high.

Reading on, it all clicked into place.

Praise God we live in unity! So we can say, "We love you whitefellas and thank God you have come to our nation."

This had to be our beloved Ma, the same tone and sentiments I had heard over the years, confirmed when I saw *Pastor Anabel* listed as the source.

Pop and Ma at the WCGIP 2000

A few days later, having crossed the Tasman Sea, I would sit at the kitchen table in Jubullum, telling Pop and Ma about our new friends in Aotearoa, and showing them the book Aunty Linda had given us. The old fella disappeared, returning with a photo in his hand. And there they were, at the *World Christian Gathering on Indigenous Peoples* in 2000, where long ago they had met the *Te Āti Awa* Aunty who, decades later, would welcome *their* godson back to *his* tribe.

It seemed a fitting final destination for the journey thus far, from Jubullum to Jordan and Jerusalem, from the palace in Honolulu to the *maraes* of Aotearoa, and back again to the place it had all begun. For it was there that a Chief who had been praying for his own indigenous ministry to be reborn, would call us to prepare *The Way* of the Lord, that his dream of old might soon come to pass.

THE DREAM

Part Four

Pop and Ma, Followers of The Way

LIKE IN THE BEGINNING

*He had been instructed
in the way of the Lord.*

Acts 18:25

They were known as followers of *The Way*.

After the life and death of Yeshua the Messiah, the movement spreading in the wake of his many signs and wonders was not called *Christianity*, nor were his disciples known as *Christians*.

At first, they were Jewish students of an Aramaic-speaking teacher from the country side, converts to a revolutionary belief system built upon the Law of Moses, but providing a path to salvation by faith alone. As the good news spread from town to town, they would welcome Greeks, Romans and people of every tongue and tribe into their midst.

It was later again, after His followers had planted communities far from Jerusalem, that the people of Antioch, a former Greek city residing in modern day Turkey, started referring to these laborers for the Lord as *Christianos*, meaning *little Christs*, said to be a subtle taunt that would survive the test of time, becoming the *Christian* of today.

When the Roman Empire adopted the emerging movement as its own, it began the process of conforming *The Way* to the structures that had served its rise as a superpower. These institutions and their leaders would oversee the workings of the church for well over a thousand years, before Martin Luther's reformation ushered in the age of a thousand and one denominations.

In the beginning, Yeshua, the prophet and preacher known to us as Jesus, had taught a framework to a life lived in loving connection with God, and others, whether friend or enemy. He had then sent his students out to share the teachings that invited everyone, no matter their rank or race, to invite the Lord into their hearts, that the glory of heaven might be revealed in their families, villages and nations.

His call was not for a religion to be run as an empire would the rest of its worldly operations, but for a revolution that would alter the course of history two common people at a time, carrying little as they traveled from house to house, and town to town. They would need no building or accessories to operate in power and achieve His mission, because wherever two or more would gather in His name, whether it be a living room, a town square, or a prison cell, He would be in their midst.

This was *The Way* of the early church, and for Pop, the boy who tasted old school revival in the 50s and 60s, the pastor who prayed for the sick and suffering through the decades to come, the elder who longed to guide even one more soul towards the light, this was the beating heart of his model for ministry.

Tent Meeting in Jubullum, 1950s

"I've been reading the Book of Acts," he said as we waited for our Indian food in Lismore, our first meal shared upon my return from overseas. Bringing a ministry back to life was at the forefront of our conversation, and I had asked if he'd given any thought as to what it might be called.

"We should call it *The Way*," he said, without a hint of hesitation. *"Like in the beginning."*

There would be steps to take and an ocean to bridge, but as to what it might be called, the Chief had spoken, and he was echoing the first followers of Yeshua, the ones who carried the torch of His teachings and the legend of His love to communities across the known world. Those they touched would blaze a path through history, until this very day that a humble elder would feel moved to raise that same

Tent Meeting for Pop and Ma's 50th Wedding Anniversary, 2016

ancient banner, calling our generation to receive a torch not bound by space or time. As in days past, it would be handed on in the simplest of ways, from old to young, from friend to friend, from rich to poor and back again, in the highways and byways, as well as from the stages, screens and pulpits of the mighty buildings of faith that dot the modern landscape.

But as Pop and the elders were trying to tell us, all the wonders of technology, with its *face* this and *insta* that, none of it seemed to compare with the way the old people used to preach and pray and praise the Lord under the trees, or down by the river. And as much as the awe-inspiring structures made of matching bricks, stone or steel appeared to reach towards the heavens, the call remained for us to be *living stones*, each one fingerprint unique, carved by the hands of the ultimate Creator into the shape he had in mind when he dreamed us into being. And then, called to pray at every corner of the globe, bonded by a love that is unbreakable, He would raise from us a temple built of human hearts, a sanctuary for the spirit of the living God to dwell. With every deep spring of the soul tapped and brought to the surface of our lives, from there would flow *rivers of living water*, the rising tide of our collective faith lifting all boats above the ways and worries of a broken world.

This was the vision for *The Way*, for any and all who hear the call to lift up the name of the Lord, to love one another and serve the needy in our midst, to break bread in homes, to pray in the parks, to learn and to live out the lessons handed down from generation to generation. From the kitchen table to the mega church, He would be among us, drawing close enough that we might hear with His ears and see with His eyes, what the size and scope of our calling might be, and with whom we might co-labor to steward our designated part of His Kingdom.

With the torch in the elders outstretched hands, and a journey to the Holy Land and the ends of the earth in the books, our calling had made itself clear, for the time had come to take an old fella's ancient dream of a ministry reborn, and to be wherever we needed to be, and to do whatever must be done, to bring his vision for *The Way* to the world.

The Mountains of Hawai'i

AT THE ENDS OF THE EARTH

And you will be my witnesses in Jerusalem, and in all Judea and Samaria, and to the ends of the earth.

Acts 1:8

Go into all the world he said.

Yeshua, the great teacher, had so impacted the lives of his students, *The Way* he taught them would burn so bright, it would spark a spiritual wildfire.

Told to remain in Jerusalem for a time, they would soon be cloaked in the power of the Holy Spirit, then sent out on journeys that would begin, and through the continual passing of the torch from one disciple to the next, never end.

I looked up at the mountains of *Oʻahu*, recalling my own time in the Old City, the stone streets that once echoed with the voices of the apostles still near and dear to my heart. But spin the globe halfway around and you find this dot of an island is about as far from Jerusalem as one can get, and if I were to honor Yeshua's final command to go and make disciples, this would be a good place to start.

At the ends of the earth.

"May the Lord richly anoint you and use you among the people," Ma had prayed, sending me back to Hawai'i with a farewell commission. "May many souls be saved, many lives be touched, A-MEN!"

That I might pass on the saving power of the gospel in my travels, was a constant prayer for Pop and Ma, that whoever I met might hear the music and the message handed down to me, as it had been to them long ago. They had spent a decade weaving *The Way* into my world, not just as a set of teachings or practices, but as a living experience of God, the faithful one who plants peace in the depths of the heart, this gift of grace beyond understanding.

Sharing that experience would be the task upon landing back in the islands, and soon the door would open to a seeker in search of this truth that had set so many free. I had landed in a share house, scheduled to stay a month, maybe two, before jetting back to Jubullum, a plan that went out the window while I watched the Lord break into the life of my housemate. In an encounter that wiped clean a lifetime of doubt, she felt the enormity and *reality* of God filling the room for the first time, growing misty eyed for months to come as she recalled the moment she said *Yes* to the knock on the door of her heart.

"Jesus makes my eyes wet," she would say, smiling.

Her life had been transformed from the inside out, and the two people she longed to thank were the ones who had done for me what I had done for her, sharing the heart of *The Way*, one old song at a time. On my next trip to Australia, I would sit with Pop

Praying for the Lord to use me among the people

and Ma on the porch in Jubullum, telling the story of the share house in Hawai'i, of how I had planned to come and go, only for the Lord to use it as a chance to bring a weary one home to Himself.

"This is for you," I said, handing them each a letter in print, the ink almost dripping with gratitude, testimony of how *The Way* had impacted this woman in a far away land, someone they had never preached to, or prayed for, but who had been touched by the torch of their ministry.

…I had a breakthrough encounter that showed me that not only was the Lord's presence felt so deeply in that moment, but that He has been with me the whole time, waiting for me to turn to Him for guidance…

Building a Bridge from Jubullum to Hawai'i

"I'm going to take this everywhere," said Pop, mightily moved by her words. "When I go and visit the other communities, I'm going to read this out for everyone to hear."

He held the paper gently in his hands, the author having blessed him in return for the blessing he had been, the letter proof that God was not just on the move, but that He was moving through the very ministry Pop was praying to life. My housemate would be the first to find the Lord through its work in the world, her story affirming the call to Hawai'i, for while *The Way* was busy being born again, it was already making disciples at the ends of the earth.

But still there was a missing link I couldn't reconcile, a mission that seemed too far stretched across the waters now separating me from the old fella. With half an ocean between us, how we would raise a ministry flag, and build a mission base, was still a mystery to me. I had assumed that Jubullum would be our ground zero, but when I brought it up with Pop, it was far from set in stone. I joked we could always set up shop in Honolulu, knowing his affection for the place, a fact I learned when he was in the hospital and I thought watching a little YouTube might raise his spirits. Told he could pick anything in the whole world to watch, he had asked for the *Marty Robbins Hawaiian Special*.

"Gee, hey," he laughed, responding to the thought of having his very own headquarters in Honolulu. "Yeah, yeah, that'd be good."

Not only had he given it consideration, he seemed to love the idea, the first hint at a growing satisfaction in knowing the spiritual torch he and Ma had kindled in their patch of the world had a role to play in places near *and* far. Pop's dream of a ministry reborn was coming into view, and though its beating heart would forever be rooted in his country and counsel, he had given a Chiefly blessing to plant a global base in our new home away from home.

There would be details to iron out, prayers to pray, and a wealth of work to be done, but *The Way* was coming to life before our eyes, and while it was blessing Pop and Ma with testimony brought to their doorstep in Jubullum, it was also building a bridge back to Honolulu and beyond, that we might be able to reach many more seekers in search of this flame the Lord Himself commissioned us to carry.

The Old Stone Church at Kawaiaha'o

THE OLD STONE CHURCH

*Your statutes have been my songs
in the house of my pilgrimage.*

Psalm 119:54 NKJV

164 days at sea.

They came from afar, trading the American Dream for a journey into the unknown, to a place of tropical mysteries, and foreign gods.

Many expected a frosty welcome, knowing the *kapu* system and its human sacrifice temples held the islands firmly in its grasp. And yet they persisted, one giant leap of faith after another, arriving off the shores of the Big Island in 1820, to shocking news.

The King was dead, the *kapu* system overthrown, the temples destroyed. Royal resistance of the sort they envisioned had given way to an opening for these bearers of the good news to stay, and share.

Wind in their spiritual sails, they taught a growing circle of students the *palapala*, introducing a written Hawaiian language to the people. Next, hot off the mission's printing press, would come *Ka Baibala Hemolele*, the Holy Bible in their native tongue.

Within decades, some 95% of the islands' inhabitants had joined the church, making Hawai'i perhaps the most Christian nation on earth. At its heart was the old stone church at *Kawaiaha'o (Ka-why-a-how)*, the now famous coral building raised as a house of prayer and worship for the Kings and Queens, and their well-adorned families of fellowship. Its rich history reminded me of two other sites with a special place in our heart, Jerusalem's *Holy Sepulchre*, and the holy ground where once stood the old church in Jubullum, the former still playing host to pilgrims in the millions, the latter long gone, but re-emerging in the hopes and prayers of *The Way*.

Our beloved ukulele-playing Uncle Doug heard my vision of taking the songs and stories of Pop and Ma around the island, and he proposed an introduction to his friend, a fellow musician. This was a man descended from famous Hawaiian preachers, who's great great great grandfather was described as the *Shepherd of the Hills*. Like his ancestor, he too had been called into church leadership, taking the role of Reverend at a well known congregation in Honolulu. He and his flock, and their sanctuary adorned with photos of the Chiefs and Chiefesses of the past, would surely be the perfect way to honor a living Chief from afar.

It was the old stone church at Kawaiaha'o.

"That's a big river," said Pop, when I told him we might have a special host in Honolulu, the crossing of the Pacific not just a bit wide for his liking, but wholly beyond his travel comfort zone. Whether the old fella made it to Hawai'i or not, doors were

Kawaiaha'o Church Still Standing in Modern Honolulu

opening and *The Way* was coming to life on its own, people and places writing themselves into a story that began at the old church in Jubullum, took a turn to the Old City's *Holy Sepulchre*, and might one day, in some way, enter the walls of *Kawaiaha'o*.

First we would follow whatever steps the Lord seemed to lay before us, going from one tent in the field to another, as we came to fellowship with families up and down the Windward Coast of *O'ahu*. In our connections and conversations, and in the songs and sermons we would hear, there seemed a longing to relive what had taken place here in the 1800s, when the gospel spread from village to village, until the islands were ablaze with the spirit of revival. And yet, one could sense the undercurrent of doubt that any such thing was possible, after what had happened in times past, the remarkable genesis

Singing the Old Songs at Kawaiaha'o in Honolulu

of the church in Hawai'i giving way to a great desertion in the decades following the overthrow of the kingdom. Some children of the original 1820 landing had been caught up on the wrong side of history, breeding distrust into the generations to come, and yet, 130 years after Lili'uokalani had been imprisoned in the palace, the descendants of those days were still singing *The Queen's Prayer*, a song of forgiveness in the throes of tragedy.

In 1866, Liliu had assumed the role of choir director and organist at *Kawaiaha'o*, the crafting of her famous musical prayer three decades later seeming to flow from a heart for worship nourished in those early days. The song would resonate through the years until my own experience at the palace, the moment I realized a three day stopover was just the opening scene to a half decade story unfolding to this day.

And what a day it would be, climbing the steps at *Kawaiahaʻo* for the first time, entering the walls of a structure who's cornerstone had been laid in 1839, greeting their beloved *Kahu*, the Reverend Kenneth Makuakāne, the one Uncle Doug had spoken of. We had crossed paths a few times, but this was the setting we had waited for, a building with a legacy to match almost any, the third of three churches making a home at the heart of our tale.

"Are you performing for us tonight?" he asked, seeing my ukulele in hand. We had gathered for the finale of the Pacific Islander and Asian American Ministries (PAMM) conference, an evening of songs and sharing by the faithful from near and far, and I had brought my instrument just in case.

"If you'll have me," I replied, a little bit surprised, knowing how stacked the schedule was, but letting him know it would be an honor. Hearing my name introduced, I stepped past the pews of old and up to the microphone, lifting my voice in the sanctuary as Liliu and so many others had in times past.

There's a river of life pouring out of me

Standing there, in the old stone church at *Kawaiahaʻo*, I would sing the songs Ma had taught me on the porch, tell of a journey from Jubullum to Jerusalem, and to these islands at the ends of the earth, offering a hearty **jingella** from the Chief of the Wahlubal on the big, big, *big* island now known as Australia, this man of great stature, who humbly bowed to the same God for whom the Kings and Queens of Hawaiʻi had built this mighty house of prayer.

jingella
hello

Keeping the Old Songs Alive, 2024

SING OUT ANOTHER CHORUS

It's an unbreakable spiritual lifeline, reaching past all appearances right to the very presence of God.

Hebrews 6:19

The drunkards cried out for another song.

It was a scene from the tattered old novel we had rescued from the free box at our local bookshop, first published in 1896, before going on to sell millions of copies. This was a page out of history that asked the the age old question: *What Would Jesus Do?*

The setting was a gospel tent in the worst part of town, flanked by drinking establishments, brothels and troublemakers of all shapes and sizes. When the singer's heavenly voice drifted into the surrounds, the people flocked to hear the hymns calling them out of a world of despair. But as the music died down, not all had ears to hear what the preacher was preaching, and a liquored up local shouted him down, demanding that they *sing out another chorus.*

I laughed when I saw his request, not only because it was wildly out of order, but because the song they suggested by name was one I had come to know myself, 125 years after the book had been written.

Throw Out The Lifeline was a country classic Pop had loved way back when, and he sang along to a *Wilburn Brothers* version we found on YouTube, while I quickly learned the chords. The next day we sat in front of the fire, singing it with Ma, who was back from the care home for the weekend. They had just prayed for my return trip to Hawai'i, clapping with joy as we closed with an old favorite brought back to life in their living room.

Landing back in the islands, I immersed myself in the repertoire handed down by the elders, a museum of melodies that could take a listener back in time, in two and a half minutes or less. But as I dreamed of pulling the soundtrack of the past into the present, I began to see their untold power to unite the faithful, across the seas and throughout the generations.

Pop and Ma had taken me to a host of Aboriginal church gatherings over the years, and I had grown accustomed to the laid back services, songs of yesteryear matched with hot-off-the-press testimony. So when we arrived to visit a Hawaiian church in *Kahalu'u*, seeing the old tent in the field felt much like coming home, and I made quick friends with the young pastor, *Ikaika*, talking story, breaking bread, and swapping songs on the ukulele and guitar.

A few weeks later, having gathered for a Wednesday night of worship and prayer, he brought out an old Hawaiian language hymn book, and I flipped through in search of some songs I might know. After running through *Softly and Tenderly, Just a Closer Walk With Thee* and a few other favorites, I turned the page and knew we had to give this one a try.

Listening to the Old Songs with Pop, 2024

Ho mai ke kaula!
Ho mai ke kaula!
Kaula o ke ola mau

Throw out the lifeline!
Throw out the lifeline!
Someone is drifting away

The song had spun its own tale, from hearing it at the kitchen table with Pop, to the scene I'd stumbled on in the novel from 1896, and now here, on an island in the heart of the Pacific, singing in two languages, delivering the same call to action that had saved thousands around the globe. That Sunday, we would sing it again under their *Hāmama Community Church* tent, closing the service with a song that had stood the test of time, a message reminding us of our duty to boldly share this lifeline of faith.

Singing the Old Songs at Home in Jubullum, 2024

For once it had saved us, and now others were reaching out for that same raft of hope that had brought us ashore. As Pop and Ma had thrown it to us, we were now being called to sail onwards through sunshine and storm, prepared at any moment to *throw out the lifeline* to a brother or sister in need, whether or not they were ready to take hold of the Lord's mighty, saving grace.

Throw out the lifeline across the dark wave
There is a brother whom someone should save

It was the greatest gift we had ever been given, one that could keep a weary head above the waves of a world crashing around us, an island of mercy in a measureless ocean whose horizon can seem so far off, it might as well stretch to the edge of eternity. We just had to throw it, Jesus, the one known here as

Iesū, would do the rest. It was a teaching Pop had brought to the table, through a record sung half a century ago, and like the others passed down from our beloved elders, it was busy laying stones for the future of *The Way.* Though we still had a ministry to launch, and a book to write, our mission to share God's love was alive in the choruses we sang every chance we got, from tent to tent and everywhere we went, tunes from another time with a mission everlasting, to soothe the soul and save the seeker.

From here to there they stood their ground as living bridges of hope, voices of many lands and languages connected by a spiritual songbook from which all were being nourished. And for us, they had fanned the flame of a story that started on the banks of the Rocky River, echoed through the Old City of Jerusalem, and landed in the fields of Hawai'i, a soundtrack that seemed to play its own starring role, each song taking turns at the wheel, taking us to destinations we wouldn't have thought to go.

Pop and Ma had sung them through thick and thin, hymns that hinted at the sound of heaven, words that lit the fire of faith in a heart called to receive. Now our generation was glimpsing their power to span seas and time, bring joy to the sorrowful and hope to the helpless, all while breathing life into a modern Chief's ancient dream to bring *The Way* to the world, one lifeline at a time.

Book scene from:
In His Steps
By Charles M. Sheldon

Easter Convention in Jubullum, 2024

AN ANCIENT DREAM REBORN

I am the resurrection and the life.

John 11:25

It was 1954 when the tent was raised.

Revival had been brought to Jubullum Village and the old people gathered from all over to sing, to pray and to praise the glorious One who's hand had lit for them a mighty spiritual fire.

For decades, Pop had held on to the dream that God would move in his community once again, his lamp of faith burning through life's trials, dimmed on occasion, but never fully losing its spark.

The old church on the mission was long gone, the prayer meetings and church rallies few and far between, baptisms in the river, once a regular sight, now fading on the horizon of his memories.

But now, a full 70 years after the tent had first gone up, Pop's vision for *The Way* was on the verge of coming true, for soon the old sports center in Jubullum would be buzzing again, the name of the resurrected One lifted up as in the days of old.

"Aloha! Aloha!" I greeted him on the phone from Hawai'i. "How are you going over there?"

"Very *very* good," came the reply, noticeably upbeat. "We're excited about what's happening in March."

"What is it?" I asked curiously, not a hint as to what he had in store.

"We're having an Easter Convention!" Pop said, his anticipation pouring through the receiver. "And you know what we're calling it…*Elders of The Way!*"

A few months earlier I had gifted him a draft of the book for Christmas, and he held it in his hands, smiling as he read out the title for the first time. Now they were preparing to host their first big church rally in decades, and Pop had felt led to name it after the story we were praying might be brought to completion before too long. But this was beyond anything we had planned to put in its pages, a leading candidate for the climax in a tale that had taken us across the seas and *back like a boomerang*, to where it had all begun, and was beginning again.

Trusting once more that the Lord would make a way out of no way, I made plans to jet back from Hawai'i, and the next thing I knew I was driving into Jubullum Village, stepping into the same old stadium where Pop had been ordained as a Reverend, where we had held his and Ma's 50th anniversary lunch, and where he had shaken the hand of the Native American Chief, almost six years ago. But this was the first time I had seen the chairs set for a gospel meeting, and as I watched the

Back at the Old Sports Center for Easter 2024

visiting aunties and uncles arrive, bringing drapes and flowers, food and guitars, you got the sense that the Spirit of God was filling the space with every hug and greeting. For those who had longed to see this day come, it was the fulfillment of a hope many had come close to losing. For those who knew little or nothing of the history being made, it was a glimpse into the power of what had been, and could be once again, if the Lord's hand truly was at work.

The services opened, and one by one they came up to worship and pray, testify and prophesy, teach and preach the gospel that had brought healing and transformation to the hearts of a countless many. This was the same message of grace and glory that once engulfed their communities across the region, a revival for the ages that had long ago laid the foundation for us to be gathered here this Easter.

The Aunties from Fire of God Church

These were the children, nieces and nephews of those who bridged the old and new worlds with the cross of Christ, the *Reconciler-in-Chief* who had called them to love others as He loves us, to enter the narrow gate and follow in the footsteps of *The Way*, wherever it might lead. Over the decades there had been some mountains too steep for weary souls to climb, and valleys that had claimed too many to mention, but here this weekend, worshipping in the wake of the ones who had prayed that a day like this might one day arrive, the Easter message seemed animated in the scenes around us, the miracle of a movement resurrected, *an ancient dream reborn*.

And for the Chief who had dreamed it into being, his words would mix expectation with responsibility, knowing the future of *The Way* would rest in the hands of the beloveds gathered before him.

"This is my river, I walk around, this is what I ask the Father for," he began. "Lord, send somebody back here to revive us, to give me strength, help me, and my community."

"For a long, long time, I walked around, people thought I was, you know," he continued, making little circles around his ear, drawing laughs from the crowd. "Sometimes they hear me, but I'm talking to somebody, I'm asking Him to do something."

"Tonight, he's showing us what he's *going* to do," his words rippled over the rows of red and gold chairs, filled with souls hungry for the kind of breakthrough we had glimpsed, at least in part, throughout these past three days. Whatever the future held, seeds of hope had been sown, and the faithful were willing to toil in prayer, that the harvest might once again be plentiful in this place.

Many had spoken prophetic words, of the spirit moving and the saints rising, of worldly chains being broken and addictions overcome, the Lord working his wonders, heart by heart, life by life. You could feel the passion pouring through the aunties and uncles as they spoke, praying the Almighty would show their lost ones how to take hold of the freedom awaiting when the darkness we try to hide is engulfed by the Lord of Lights, and washed away by these stripes of His, the ones that heal all wounds.

"You came here to be a start of this," Pop spoke pointedly. "Don't go away and forget it."

"You're in it now, you're a partner now."

Still basking in the glow of what had taken place over the weekend, Pop would record a recap of the event to take back to our friends across the sea.

"We have just concluded our *Elders of The Way* Easter Convention in Jubullum," he began. "It's been a wonderful time with the gathering of many who came from different parts of the area."

"They were singing, sharing testimonies and waving banners," Pop continued. "Evangelist Alf Green then brought forth the message *Nothing Is Impossible With God*, while many people came forward for prayer, a fresh touch, a fresh anointing, and for healing."

They truly had come from all over to participate, some from hundreds of miles, lifting their voices in one accord as the old hymns echoed off the walls, the goodness of God declared for all to hear. And there was Pop and Ma, side by side in the front row, still kicking after 46 years in ministry and 58 years of marriage, witnessing the fruit of their prayers, the fulfillment of a desire for the saints to gather again in the village where their story had started so long ago.

It is finished, the battle is over
It is finished, and Jesus is Lord

What a sight to see flags of every color waving in worship as Uncle Peter Walker sang out with his booming voice on Sunday morning, all in the hall arising to celebrate the risen Lord, the Mighty One who saves, the Holy One we serve. Witnesses to a window you would need the hand of God to open, you could feel the fire swirling among the people

It is Finished, the Battle is Over

gathered, a power that could bring peace to the one and the many, if given the chance. That now would be the quest, for what had become *Elders of The Way* was emerging as a platform to share the story of stories, the songs of the saints, and the saving power of the gospel, the one that wins the battle for the human heart every time it's received.

From Jubullum to Jerusalem, and to the ends of the earth, we would do our best to serve the will of the Almighty, following His signs along the path, that our steps might lead to a harvest far beyond our own making. And in the meantime, we would trust for many more miracles as His plans took shape, for though the Easter Convention of 2024 had been one for the ages, it was safe to assume the Resurrected One wasn't finished with us yet.

Uncle Wayne in Hawai'i, 2024

FIRST ACROSS THE BRIDGE

Blessed are those whose strength is in you, whose hearts are set on pilgrimage.

Psalm 84:5

All it took was a ukulele and four boomerangs.

Our story that had jumped from Jubullum to Jerusalem, had made itself a home in Hawai'i, and the call had gone back across the sea, planting the seed of pilgrimage in the elders of *The Way*.

Uncle Wayne would be *first across the bridge*.

He had stopped by to visit Pop one day, grabbing his ukulele from the car to cheer him up with a few of the old favorites. But inside he felt there was more to do, and after praying with Vera, his beloved wife of 45 years, he went back to see if the old fella wanted them to plan a special weekend.

The Easter Convention of 2024.

I had sat with Uncle Wayne over the big weekend, telling him of the doors opening for us in the islands, and how God seemed to be building a bridge from the Rocky River to the kingdom of *aloha*.

"I want to come visit," he said without hesitation, even though he'd never left Australia and didn't have a passport, let alone money for a ticket. But what he did have in droves was the faith of his elders, and his trust in the Lord gave him all the peace he needed to find provision for the unknown.

"I just felt something in my heart calling me to go," he would say later. "I made some boomerangs, took them down to the shop, and they bought them all! Then I felt the Lord saying to take the money and go straight to buy a plane ticket, so I did."

As Easter drew to a close, he had sent me back to Hawai'i with four boomerangs, hand painted gifts for our friends across the sea. The first I would present to the big fella, our dear Uncle Kaneala, as an invitation to join us on a journey back to Jubullum. Another would go to the old stone church at *Kawaiaha'o* in Honolulu, after I'd sung and shared the story of Pop and Ma, *there's a River of Life pouring out of me* echoing throughout the famous coral building raised for the Kings and Queens of Hawai'i. Still another had gone to *Ka 'Ohana O Ke Aloha,* our Hawaiian church family that had sent me off at Easter with gifts, songs and prayers for Pop and Ma, five years after hosting the once-a-year event that had miraculously drawn me in on my very first day in the islands.

"You should come for *Ho'olohe Pono,*" I had told Uncle Wayne, sharing my experience of that event, the name calling us to *listen well, rightly, carefully* to the native people of the land. It would seem like something out of a dream, but there he was, an

Uncle Wayne at Hoʻolohe Pono, 2024

Aboriginal elder from a country town in the hills, stepping out of the International Arrivals at Honolulu Airport. With a welcome *lei* around his neck and steel guitar on the stereo, we drove across *Oʻahu*, mountain peaks rising from ocean to sky, waves of *aloha* greeting him as we arrived for church by the beach in *Waimānalo*, our friends excited to fellowship with this uncle from afar. To honor his arrival, and the old fella who had sent him as his representative, we got the whole tent singing in Wahlubal, the first song I'd learned with Pop and Ma, the one we'd sung at every other turn.

Ngai Yoway, Yoway, Yoway
Ngai Yoway, Yoway, Yoway
Ngai Yoway Marmung
Ngai Yoway Marmung
Ngai Yoway, Yoway, Yoway

Uncle Wayne with his "cuz" Uncle Kaneala

Uncle Wayne was called to the mic and he shared about the countryside back home, the turtle divers of the Rocky, the challenges they had faced as a people, and the grace of a loving God who carried them through every kind of storm. As the week unfolded, we met morning and night at sites across the island, making friends for life and listening intently to the stories and struggles of our hosts. Time and again, Uncle Wayne's words would bridge the Hawaiian and Aboriginal experiences, honoring their shared journeys of life and loss, and making it known how inspired he had become to double his efforts when he got back home.

On the final day we arrived at ʻIolani Palace, where I had first met this fellowship family five years ago. Entering the *Imprisonment Room*, I stood in the very spot I had that first week in Hawaiʻi, listening to our friends sing *The Queen's Prayer* once again, reflecting on how much had happened from one hearing to the next. We had seen the fulfillment of Pop's dream at Easter, a ministry and movement taking shape, and a book that had almost written itself to honor their legacy and carry their candle of faith to the world.

And then there was this Uncle standing next to me, the one who had never left the shores of Australia, who had played his ukulele to cheer up the old fella, not knowing it would be his ticket to visit the very birthplace of the instrument that started it all. And the final of the four boomerangs he had given me to bring back at Easter, Uncle Wayne was able to present in person to a legendary Hawaiian elder on the West Side of O'ahu, a farewell gift as the sun set on a week we would never forget.

With what seemed like a closing chapter in the books, our task would be connecting the dots from the islands where our story had landed, back to the Aboriginal village where it had begun, perhaps even retracing our tracks to the Old City of Jerusalem, where Yeshua the Messiah had commissioned His followers to go into all the world, proclaiming the Kingdom of Heaven at hand.

But first, we would call our new friends in Hawai'i on a journey to the source of *this* story, to meet the great Poppy Harry Mundine Walker, his beloved Annabelle, and their brothers and sisters, nieces and nephews, cousins, colleagues and friends in the Lord, mighty servants who had been raised to resurrect the power of the old church, seven decades after revival had lit the flame of faith in their region.

God willing, our friends from afar would stand with us on the foundations of the old church and the banks of the Rocky River, joining us as witnesses to *an ancient dream reborn,* the raising of a ministry drawn from the heart of the elders, a message of old with a mission for the future.

Together we would pray for the Lord to move as he had in Jubullum in the 1950s and Honolulu in the 1800s, indeed as he had in the beginning, when the torch of *The Way* was first lit, a heavenly fire handed down for 2,000 years, ready as ever to spark the hearts of a willing generation, those of us from many nations, divided by seas, but united in the quest to see the Lord light up the world, one heart at a time.

From there we would gather where we might be called next, from house to house and church to church, in living rooms and tents, in city parks and halls, casting seeds for harvest as in the early days, when the faithful welcomed seekers and saints of any sort, inviting them to break bread, to pray, and to let this Lord they loved into their hearts. And with Pop's relentless encouragement, we would emerge with a story of two saints and their godson, of a *calling* to serve, a *torch* passed on, a *journey* over the seas, and an old fella's *dream* come true.

So it is from here that we set sail for whatever is to come, praying for the one and the many to be called out of the world, to remember how things were and could be again, if only we still ourselves long enough for the pages of history to turn themselves as they once did, not by our will or by our works, but by the power of His own mighty hands.

Pop and Ma, Elders of The Way, 2023

For with the wave of one, he can pour heavenly sunshine on an ancient tribe, raise a holy city from a desert valley, and weave a *lei* of stars across the sky. With it too he can make a prayer warrior from a hungry Aboriginal girl, a Reverend and a Chief from a humble mission boy, and bring them a servant and student tasked with taking their tale to the globe.

And with the other, He reaches out to the weak and the weary, whatever we've done, wherever we've been, it matters no more for His presence brings peace, His might moves mountains, our freedom in Him giving us faith to face all fear, hope to conquer helplessness, and courage to say *Yes* to the candle of His love burning brightly in our hearts, that the rays of His lighthouse might shine upon our path, this precious one paved by the *Elders of The Way*.

THE END

THE

Your ears will hear a voice behind you, saying, "This is the way; walk in it."

ISAIAH 30:21

~~~

A gift opens the way and ushers the giver into the presence of the great.

PROVERBS 18:16

~~~

Teach me, Lord, the way of your decrees, that I may follow it to the end.

PSALM 119:33

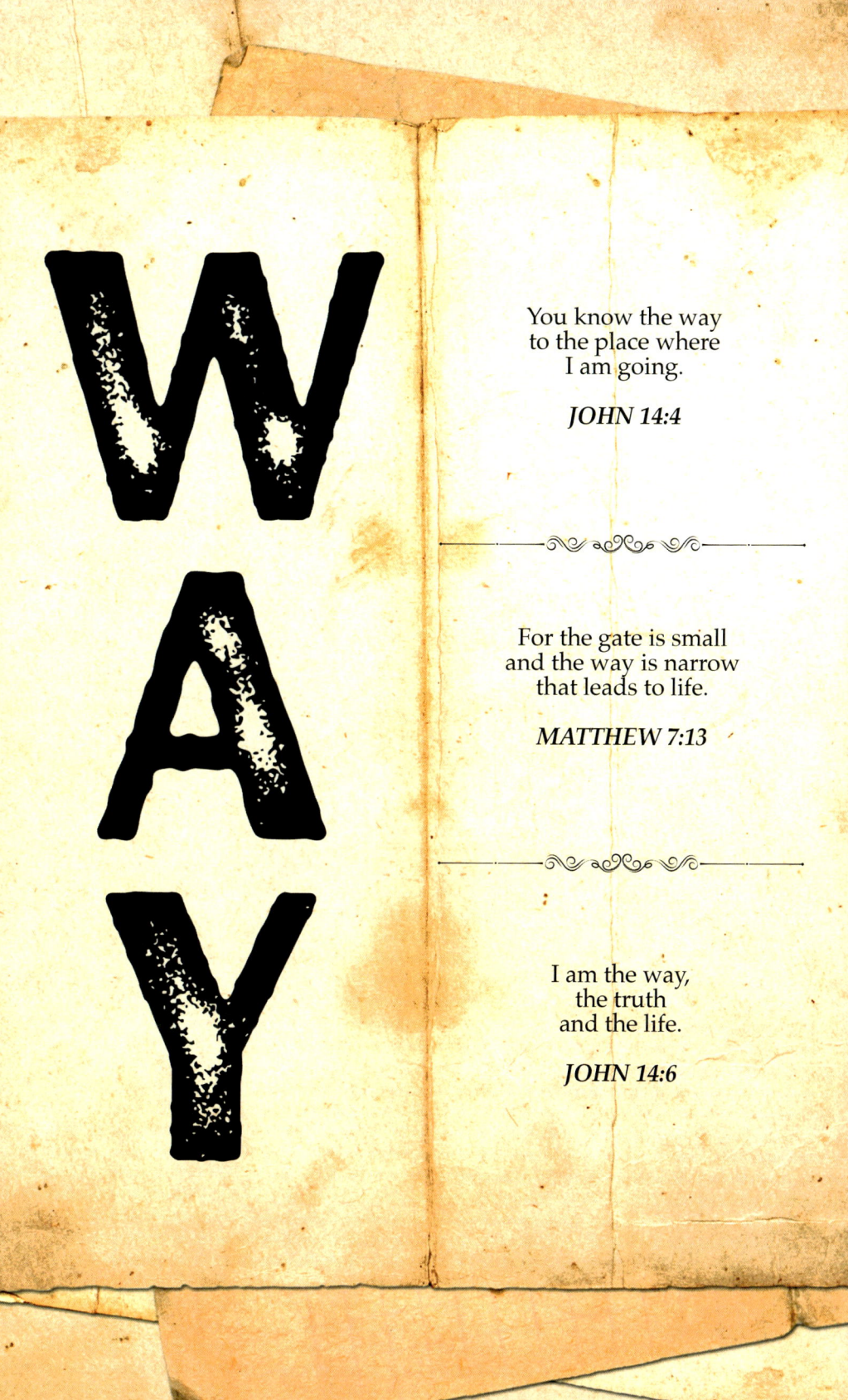

MESSAGE FROM POP

POPPY HARRY MUNDINE WALKER

I just want to pass on a few verses of scripture, what the Master, the Messiah, the Lord Jesus Christ, the Anointed One, is to me. Not only to me, but to you too. He loves you, he wants to bless you, and he wants to strengthen you in your walk of Christian life.

For me, the Lord is my light and my salvation. He is the the light of my life and he is the light of your life too. He is my salvation and he is your salvation too. He's the strength of my life, of your life, not only our Protector, but our Savior, our Redeemer and our Healer.

In all what he is to me and means to me is yours too. He loves you, he loves me, he cares for you, he cares for me. For God is love, God cares for us. May the blessing of our Lord be upon you and upon your land. Amen.

The Lord is my light and my salvation; whom shall I fear? The Lord is the strength of my life; of whom shall I be afraid?

PSALM 27:1

MESSAGES FROM MA

AUNTY ANNABELLE WALKER

Hallelujah! Praise the Lord! Glory be to God! We praise God that He lives and is looking over us. Out there loved one, God loves you, God cares for you, and our God is an answer to our needs and our prayers.

I remember when God would call me I said "No", but once I said "Yes!" and I never looked back. He changed me and made me into a better person. He CHOSE me, and he SAVED me. A-MEN!

I love God so much because he loves me, he loves all of us, and he breaks down the barriers and makes us one.

Lord, I thank you for the blood that flows from Calvary, that covers us and keeps us safe.

Thank you for providing for us Lord. We worship you, we exalt you, and we claim the fruit of praise upon our lips.

FROM THE HEART OF REVIVAL
1954 - 1978

A powerful move of God sweeps through the Aboriginal churches of the Northern Rivers in the 1950s and 60s. Jubullum Village welcomes visitors from near and far, baptizing new believers in the nearby Rocky River.

From the heart of revival, young Harry Walker and his newlywed Annabelle begin what will become a 50 year journey as Christian pastors, preachers and elders throughout the region.

After Harry's graduation from Bible College in 1978, he and Annabelle move into ministry as pastors of the Uniting Church in South Lismore, Australia where they serve the community for close to a decade.

AN ANCIENT DREAM REBORN

1992 - 2024

In 1992, Harry is ordained as the first Aboriginal Uniting Church Reverend in the state of New South Wales, as he and Annabelle extend their ministry up and down the east coast of Australia.

In 2016, Harry and Annabelle celebrate their 50th wedding anniversary with a gospel meeting on the site of the old church in Jubullum, sowing seeds for a ministry to emerge on the foundations of the past.

In 2024, 70 years after the revival tent was first raised, Poppy Harry's dream of a ministry reborn is realized through the Elders of The Way Easter Convention in Jubullum, with a base in Hawai'i carrying the torch to the world.

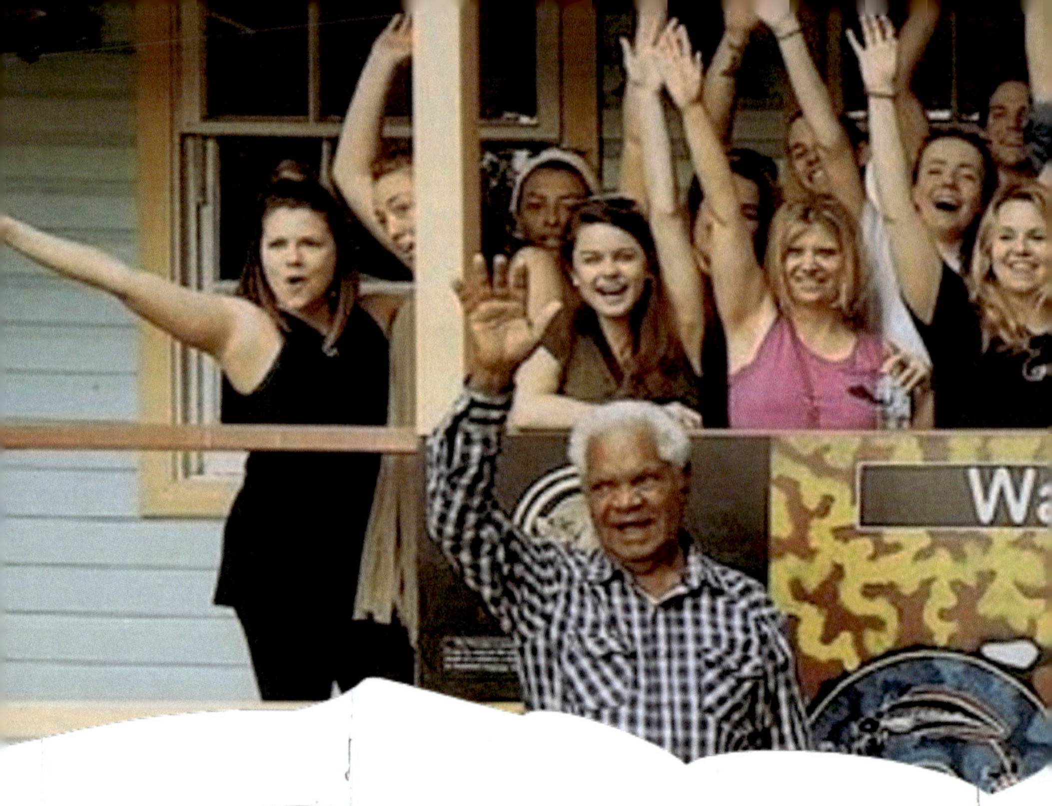

VISIT THE *Website*

- PRAYER NETWORK
- BOOKS & RESOURCES
- SHARE YOUR STORY
- NEWS & EVENTS
- CONTACT INFO

How good and pleasant it is when God's people live together in unity!

PSALM 133:1

FROM ONE HOUSE OF PRAYER TO ANOTHER

Join us in friendship and fellowship

From one house of prayer to another, wherever you are and whatever your background, we give thanks to God that we might be connected in the ways He has planned for us. May the Almighty richly bless you, your families, and the places you call home.

eldersoftheway.com

THE PRAYERS *to finish*

Anoint this book

Gee, that's nice!

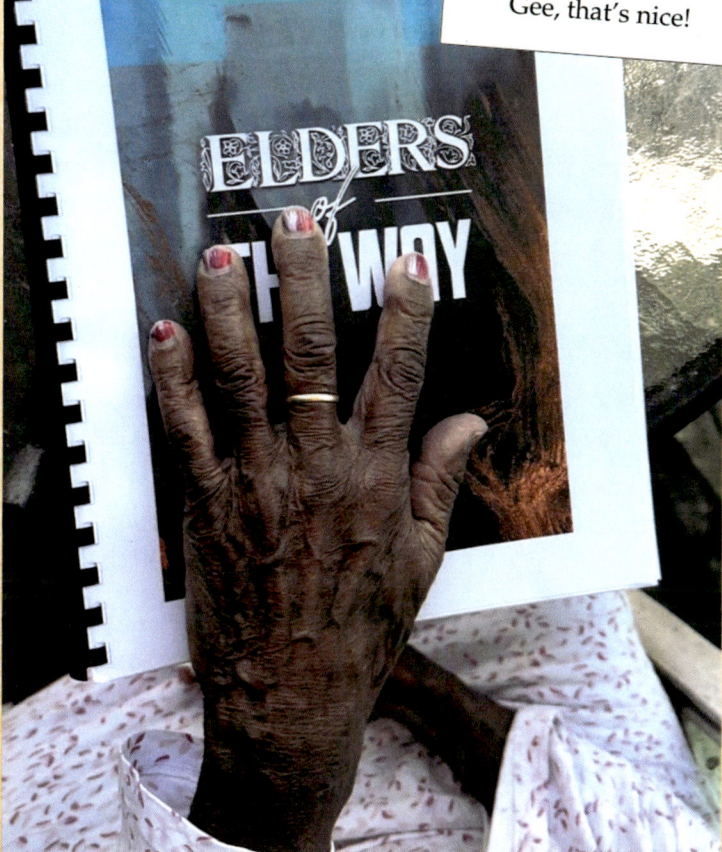

You should get these made up for everyone - Ma

1 Hear me, Lord, and answer me,
   for I am poor and needy.
2 Guard my life, for I am faithful to you;
   save your servant who trusts in you.
   You are my God;
3 have mercy on me, Lord,
   for I call to you all day long.
4 Bring joy to your servant, Lord,
   for I put my trust in you.
5 You, Lord, are forgiving and good,
   abounding in love to all who call to you.
6 Hear my prayer, Lord;
   listen to my cry for mercy.
7 When I am in distress, I call to you,
   because you answer me.
8 Among the gods there is none like you, Lord;
   no deeds can compare with yours.
9 All the nations you have made
   will come and worship before you, Lord;
   they will bring glory to your name.
10 For you are great and do marvelous deeds;
    you alone are God.
11 Teach me your way, Lord,
    that I may rely on your faithfulness;
    give me an undivided heart,
    that I may fear your name.
12 I will praise you, Lord my God, with all my heart;
    I will glorify your name forever.

Psalm 86:1-12

www.ingramcontent.com/pod-product-compliance
Lightning Source LLC
Chambersburg PA
CBRC091934130526
44582CB00047B/172